THE CHRISTIAN YEAR

THE
CHRISTIAN
YEAR

J.C.J. METFORD

THAMES AND HUDSON

GILLIAN   STEPHEN
SAMUEL   DOROTHEA   VERITY
filiae generi nepotibus dilectissimis

Printed and bound in Yugoslavia

Contents

Preface

THIS BOOK IS INTENDED AS A COMPANION FOR those who observe, or are interested in, the annual round of the ecclesiastical year. The aim is threefold: to discuss origins; to give reasons; and to suggest the theological justification for festivals which in some instances have proved controversial. It is therefore primarily explanatory rather than devotional, and ecumenical in intent. The modest hope is to promote sympathetic understanding amongst all who appreciate the importance of the Christian year in worship.

The calendar of the *Roman Missal*, the culmination of reforms initiated by the Second Vatican Council (1962–65), is the norm because it is inclusive and because many other Churches which have accomplished similar revisions approximate to it. Within the Anglican Communion the *Book of Common Prayer*, as John Keble stated in *The Christian Year* (1827), offers 'a sober standard of feeling in matters of practical religion'. His poems demonstrate the depth of devotion which the observance of holy days and seasons inspires. The *American Prayer Book* (1979) and the *Alternative Service Book* (1980) are cited for similar reasons.

Although much has been done to simplify liturgical language, there remain many technical words and phrases which require explanation. These are defined where they first occur and etymologies, where applicable, are given. Further information is included in the glossary. Reference is made to music and works of art which relate to the great festivals.

I express my thanks to those who have assisted and encouraged me. The Reverend Peter Cobb, Vicar of All Saints' Church, Clifton, Bristol, generously allowed me to pillage his library and to profit from his liturgical expertise. My daughter, Dr Gillian Clark, guided me to valuable references and early texts. Mr Eric Hancock meticulously prepared the typescript. As always throughout our long years together Edith, my wife, provided the domestic calm and intellectual companionship which made writing this book a pleasure.   *Bristol. Pentecost. 1990*

Abbreviations

Other Abbreviations

AV Authorized Version of the Bible. *b.* born. BVM Blessed Virgin
Mary. *c.* circa (approximately). *c.d.* canonized. *d.* died. *f.d.* feast day.
St Saint. Vg Vulgate version of the Bible

Notes

1. Biblical references are given as Lk (Luke) 2 (Chapter 2):4–7 (verses
   four to seven).
2. Psalms are numbered as Ps (Psalm) 95 (Hebrew number)/94 (Vulgate
   number).
3. Dates are AD unless specified as BC.
4. The dates for popes and emperors represent the years of their papacy
   or reign.
5. The following are the principal Service Books to which reference is
   made: *Roman Missal* 1970, *Book of Common Prayer* 1662, *The
   Alternative Service Book* 1980, *The American Prayer Book* 1979.

Origins

ELIGIOUS LEADERS OF THE ISRAELITES WHO had settled in the land of Canaan transformed the rite, common among nomadic shepherds, of sprinkling lamb's blood on their tent-pegs to ward off evil spirits, into the annual commemoration of God's merciful intervention when he freed his chosen people from bondage in Egypt. At supper on the last day before the full moon which followed the spring equinox, families recalled, as they do today, the events of the exodus when their ancestors were ordered to smear the doorposts and lintels of their dwellings with lamb's blood as a sign to the avenging angel to 'pass over' and spare their firstborn sons. They consumed a ritually slaughtered lamb, roasted and flavoured with bitter herbs, and for seven days ate unleavened bread, the farmer's way to avoid mixing flour from the old grain with the new, but explained as the bread made without yeast which the fugitives took with them in their hasty departure. Fifty days later, the end of the grain harvest, at the feast of the first fruits, the nation joyfully thanked God for his bounty.

In the year 30 of the present era, at the time of the Passover celebrations, Jesus of Nazareth was crucified on the orders of Pontius Pilate, Roman prefect of the ancient Jewish kingdom of Judaea and Governor of Jerusalem. On the day of Pentecost (a word derived from the Greek for 'the fiftieth'), Jesus' followers, who accepted him as the promised Christ (Greek *christos*, translating the Hebrew for 'Messiah': 'anointed one') were filled with the spirit of God. Enthused, they began to proclaim the good tidings that, through the life, death and resurrection of Jesus, the Christ, the salvific reign of God was present and at work in the world.

The fundamental symbolism and basic structure of the Christian liturgical year originated in the fact, perceived to be divinely ordained, that these decisive events coincided with Jewish festivals. There was also another coincidence: Jesus rose from the dead on the first day of the Jewish week which was based on the sabbath, a day when work ceased because, after creating the world in six days, God rested (Hebrew *shabât*) on the seventh. The day of Jesus' resurrection, the day after the sabbath, was therefore the eighth day, the beginning of the new creation, the inauguration of 'the end time' which would culminate in the return of Jesus Christ and the radical transformation of the universe. Christians, 'votaries of Christ', a name first given to them at Antioch within a decade of the resurrection, therefore placed the day after the sabbath at the centre of their religious observance. This is the origin of the weekly assembly, attendance at which distinguishes Christians from adherents of other faiths.

The Lord's Day

A late-fourth-century text, bearing the name of Addai, reputed founder of the Christian community at Edessa (Urfa, in Asiatic Turkey), explained why they came together on the first day of the week. It said, 'the apostles decided that on the day after the sabbath there would be the assembly, the reading of the holy books and the offering of the eucharist, because on that day Christ rose from the dead, and it will be again on that day that he will appear to us at the end, accompanied by his angels'. When this would be had not been revealed but, in accordance with their belief in the symbolic parallelism of the events in Christ's perfect life, Christians hoped that he would return at the same hour as he rose from the dead, before dawn on the day after the sabbath when his rock-tomb was found to be empty.

The Jewish day began with the appearance of the moon and ended the next evening. Christians therefore assembled after sunset, when the sabbath had ended, for the study of the scriptures, prayer and praise. Towards midnight they began their communal meal, the central act of which was the eucharist (from the Greek for 'giving of thanks') when the one who presided 'gave thanks' and 'broke the bread', a ritual gesture which recalled what Jesus did at supper on the night that he was betrayed to the Temple authorities. At that moment Jesus became sacramentally present, as he was at the house in Emmaus when two disciples recognized their risen Lord 'in the breaking of the bread' (Lk 24:30). One of the few phrases in Aramaic, the Semitic language spoken in Jesus' day, which survived among Greek-speaking Christians, an indication that it was of primitive liturgical origin, was *maranatha*: 'the Lord comes', which could also mean, 'Our Lord, come!', either interpretation being expressive of the reality of Christ's presence in the eucharist and of the confident expectation of his promised return.

In these contexts 'Lord' had profound theological implications. The periphrasis in Hebrew scriptures for the unutterable name of God was rendered as *kyrios*: 'Lord' in the Septuagint, the Greek version consulted by the first Christians. Applied to Jesus after his exaltation to the right hand of God, it meant that he had been given God's own name, 'which is above all other names'. He was thus superior to 'all beings in the heavens, on earth and in the underworld' (Ph 2:9–10) and infinitely greater than Roman emperors who had appropriated the title 'lord'.

In their public documents and in converse with those who used the Judaic lunar calendar, Christians spoke of 'the first day of the week', but among themselves it was 'the Lord's Day', a phrase which was certainly current towards the end of the first century. It appears in *The Revelation to John* (c.95 in its final form) where John, imprisoned on the island of Patmos, informed his fellow Christians on the Asiatic mainland that he was in a state of ecstasy 'on the Lord's Day' when he experienced his visions (Rv 1:10). In *The Teaching of the Twelve Apostles*, a didactic compilation, parts of which may belong to the same period, Christians were admonished to come together, 'on the Lord's Day, instituted by the Lord'. Some years later, Ignatius, bishop of Antioch, on his way to martyrdom in Rome, commended Christians living near Ephesus who no longer kept the sabbath but ordered their lives by 'the Lord's Day, the day when life first dawned for us'.

Sunday

Independent confirmation that the eucharistic assembly on the Lord's Day was firmly established by the end of the first century as the focus of Christian worship comes from the report on suspected subversive activities at Pontus, part of a Roman province bordering the Black Sea, which Pliny the Younger, special commissioner, sent c.112 to his patron, the Emperor Trajan. From relapsed members of the community, he elicited the information that Christians met 'on a fixed day before dawn . . . to sing a hymn to Christ as to a god'. (The second part of this quotation is open to various interpretations.) Pliny could not be precise as to the day because, although Romans had 'market-days' at approximately eight-day intervals, they had no week as such, nor official means of naming, as opposed to dating, a particular day. Unofficially, a recurrent cycle of seven days, of Egyptian origin according to the Roman historian Dio Cassius (c.150–235), was coming into use as a measurement of time in lands bordering the

Mediterranean. Each day was named after one of the seven celestial bodies – Sun, Moon, Mars, Mercury, Jupiter, Venus and Saturn – which controlled its first hour. Germanic tribes in contact with Roman civilization adopted this system, retaining the dedications to the Sun, Moon and Saturn but substituting Nordic deities – Tyr (or Ziu), Wotan, Thor (or Donar) and Freia – for the other four planetary days. English names for days of the week were derived from these ascriptions.

Addressing his *Apology* (*c*.155), a defence of the faith for which he died, to the Emperor Marcus Aurelius 'and the whole Roman people', Justin (St Justin Martyr) used the Roman seven-day sequence in which Saturn's day corresponded to the sabbath and Sun's day to the first day of the Jewish week. He explained that Christians met on Sunday because 'Jesus was crucified before that of Saturn and on the day after, which is Sun's day, he appeared to his apostles and disciples'.

At this period, and for some time afterwards, Christians were thought of as enemies of the state, subject to seizure of their property and sporadic persecutions. They achieved the status of a tolerated religion under the Emperor Constantine (*d*.337) who, although not baptized until he was near death, favoured the Christian cause. Like his father before him, he was nevertheless a devotee of *Sol invictus*: 'the unconquered Sun', protector of his empire. In 321, to provide a day of rest and recreation for his soldiers, he decreed that, 'on the revered day of the Sun', the law courts should be closed and townsfolk and artisans should cease work. (Agricultural workers were exempt in order to take advantage of weather favourable to sowing cereals and planting vines.)

This legislation indirectly benefitted Christians, making it unnecessary for them to conclude their Sunday meeting before dawn, when work began. Laws passed in the time of the Emperor Theodosius I (379–95), when Christianity had become the sole permitted religion, prohibited public entertainments on Sundays and set the pattern for the protection, throughout the centuries, of Sunday as the day for worship and recreation, free from all but essential employment.

The Saviour's Passover

References to the weekly assembly in the earliest Christian documents, letters written *c*.56–61 by Paul, 'little one', the Roman name of Saul of Tarsus, a converted rabbinic scholar, are few and incidental because common practice was then taken for granted, but they are sufficient to show that there was general acceptance of Sunday, the Roman equivalent of the first day of the Jewish week, as the day for the eucharistic gathering. Thus Paul could request Christians at the notorious seaport of Corinth and those of the faith in Galatia, the Roman province in modern central Turkey, to set aside money for the relief of the poor in Jerusalem 'on the first day of the week' (I Cor 16:1–2). In the eye-witness account of one of Paul's missionary journeys, included in *Acts of the Apostles* (c.70?), it was recorded that at Troas, a port near the site of ancient Troy, 'on the first day of the week when we met for the breaking of bread', Paul preached far into the night, with unfortunate consequences for a youth called Eutychus, who was overcome by heat and sleep and fell from an upper storey to the courtyard below (Ac 20:7–12).

In contrast to this universal acceptance of Sunday was the divergence of opinion as to the day on which the annual commemoration of the death and resurrection of Jesus should fall. Asian churches, following the tradition in the *Gospel of John* that Jesus died when the Passover lambs were slaughtered in the Temple, insisted on keeping the fourteenth day of the Jewish month Nisan, the first month of the religious year, and for this reason they became known as *Quartodecimans*: 'fourteeners'. As this date, dependent on the first full moon sighted after the spring equinox, could fall on different days of the week, Quartodecimans had often ended their fast while others who – if indeed they observed at that time an annual festival – insisted that it should always be on a Sunday, were still fasting.

This was the anomaly which St Polycarp, bishop of Smyrna, shortly before his martyrdom c.155–6 discussed with Anicetus, who then occupied the chair of St Peter at Rome. He claimed, with some justification, that the Quartodeciman practice was of apostolic institution. (At his trial he confessed that he had served the Lord for eighty-six years, probably meaning 'since baptism', so that he might well have encountered John the Apostle who was reputed to have died at Ephesus at an advanced age.) The bishops agreed to accept the validity of their respective traditions. St Victor I (189–98) was not so accommodating. Confronted by Blastus, a Quartodeciman presbyter in Rome, he obtained from local synods and councils a majority in favour of Sunday, despite the impressive list of bishops and martyrs, going back to apostolic days, which Polycrates, bishop of Ephesus, produced in support of 14 Nisan.

Victor threatened those who opposed him with excommunication: Irenaeus, bishop of Lyons, true to his name which means 'peace-maker', urged moderation. The sentence, if imposed, was ineffective because

Quartodecimans, who eventually formed a separate Church, persisted in their observance of 14 Nisan well into the fifth century. Other Churches eventually agreed that the Saviour's Passover should always be commemorated on the Sunday following 14 Nisan, or if this were a Sunday, then the next, a solution which commended itself to those who wished to distance themselves from Jewish customs. This did not settle the question of date, which continued for centuries to be controversial.

One problem arose from the need to co-ordinate the variable lunar date of 14 Nisan with the civil solar calendar perfected by Julius Caesar. In some years it was possible for many to be fasting before the festival while others were celebrating, an anomaly which, according to the *Life of Constantine*, attributed to Eusebius, bishop of Caesarea, prompted the emperor to order that the Saviour's Passover should everywhere be kept on the same Sunday, after the 25 March, the vernal equinox in the Julian calendar. Another difficulty was the need to produce a table which would correlate lunar months with solar years, taking into account the need to intercalate months, and to produce a cycle of years when, after a period, the month and the year would attain the same relative position.

Fragments of a statue, now in the Vatican Library, found in 1551 in the Via Tiburtina, Rome, revealed that St Hippolytus (*c*.170–*c*.236) had tried to solve this problem, for tables incised on the side panels of his philosopher's chair showed a sixteen-year cycle, soon found to be erroneous. Opponents of the appointment to the See of Rome of Symmachus (498–514) complained that he was unfitted for office because he kept the Saviour's Passover according to a 532-year cycle computed by Victorius of Aquitaine. A more exact and acceptable nineteen-year cycle was drawn up by Dionysius (*c*.525), called Exiguus, 'the short', a Scythian monk resident in Rome. This was the table used by St Augustine, first archbishop of Canterbury, when he and his monks began the conversion of the Anglo-Saxon kingdom of Kent in the summer of 597.

Easter

Passover in Latin is *pascha*, from which is derived the English noun 'pasc' and the adjective 'paschal', but the name for the festival in English is 'Easter' which the Venerable Bede (*c*.673–735), historian of the English Church, in his encyclopaedic work on chronology, explained as falling in *Easturmonath*: 'Easter month', so called after the goddess Ēostre, a deity difficult to identify in Germanic mythology. As Bede was disposed to fanciful etymologies, there is no reason to accept his derivation of Easter, a word which may be connected with the east, the direction of the rising sun.

St Augustine and his successors strove to persuade the bishops of the Celtic Church, which had survived in Ireland and the north and west of Britain, to accept the Roman date of Easter, but they refused, claiming that the date in the calendar which they erroneously attributed to Anatolius (*d.c.*282), bishop of Laodicea, was the correct one. The matter was debated at the Synod of Whitby (664) before King Oswin of Northumbria. Brought up in the Celtic tradition in the monastery of Iona, off the west coast of Scotland, he found that in some years he was celebrating Easter while Eanfelda, his Kentish-educated queen, was keeping the fast which followed Palm Sunday. If Eddius Stephanus of Ripon is correct, his master, Wilfrid (634–709), argued the Roman case so successfully that the king agreed, saying, 'with a smile', that, as St Peter held the keys of heaven, it was better to be on his side.

The appointment of Theodore of Tarsus (602–90), a Greek monk, to the See of Canterbury led to the adoption of the Roman date in southern England but Celtic bishops did not conform until the ninth century. Roman usage prevailed after the reorganization which followed the Norman conquest in 1066. Priests were trained to calculate the date of Easter in accordance with the method shown in the table later included in the *Book of Common Prayer*. A medieval legend relates that, in answer to the prayers of an unlettered cleric, unable to comprehend these intricacies, the font in his church was miraculously filled with water in time for baptisms at the paschal festival!

In the West, Easter may be as early as 21 March or as late as 25 April, a variation which affects the penitential season of Lent and the great festivals of Ascension and Pentecost. Although it would be a break with tradition, many Churches would be prepared to accept a fixed Easter, possibly on the Sunday nearest to 7 April, the probable date of the crucifixion in the year 30. This would mean no more than a week's variation, with consequential pastoral and social benefits.

The Great Fifty Days

In the Holy Land, cereals sown in mid-October, during the rainy season, were harvested in the spring from mid-March onwards. A sheaf of barley, the first crop to be gathered at the time of the feast of Unleavened Bread, was brought by men of the family to the Temple in Jerusalem where the priest waved it in the sanctuary, a ritual gesture, offering it to the Lord God in thanksgiving for the harvest. After forty-nine days, when wheat and the earliest tree fruits had ripened, they celebrated the completion of the in-gathering at 'the festival which follows a week of weeks' (in Hebrew *Shabu-ôt*), known to Greek-speaking Jews as Pentecost (from the Greek *he pentēkostē*: 'the fiftieth'). Opinion was nevertheless divided as to the day from which this fifty-day period should be computed. The point at issue was the interpretation of the word 'sabbath' in the text which ordered that the first sheaf of barley should be offered 'on the day after the sabbath' (Lv 23:11).

Some sects, notably the community at Qumrân who left the Dead Sea scrolls and who followed the solar calendar of the *Book of Jubilees*, which may have been composed by one of their number *c*.140–100 BC, as well as the powerful Sadducean party who controlled Temple finances, held that in this instance 'sabbath' meant Passover. Pharisees, 'the separated ones', zealous for the Law, understood 'sabbath' literally and argued that the seven weeks should be counted from the first sabbath after Passover, so that Pentecost would fall on the day after the sabbath, the Christian Lord's Day. It is not known which interpretation was accepted by the first Christians but in either case Pentecost was 'a holy convention' when servile tasks were forbidden (Nb 28:26). This would explain why, instead of departing for work at dawn, they were still in session 'at the third hour of the day' (9 a.m.) when the Holy Spirit descended upon them (Ac 2:1–13).

There was a rabbinic tradition that Moses ascended Mount Sinai fifty days after the first Passover which followed the exodus from Egypt. Thus, as well as being a harvest festival, Pentecost also commemorated 'the giving of the Law' (in Hebrew *Matan Torah*) when devout Jews spend the night studying holy writ. The flashes of lightning which accompanied the manifestation of the Lord God on that occasion were seen by Christians to presage the 'tongues of fire' which came to rest on the heads of those who received the Holy Spirit. For them Pentecost therefore meant the granting of the new law, Christ's law of love. Furthermore, it was stated in the *Book of Jubilees* that it was ordained in the holy tablets which Moses received on Mount Sinai that the feast of Weeks should be celebrated each year, so that the eternal covenant which God made with Noah and his sons would be perpetuated. If, as may well be the case, Christians knew this book, then for them Pentecost may also have represented the renewal of the old covenant (also translated as 'testament' in their early writings) and its final confirmation in the new, sealed by the blood of Christ.

The earliest reference to the annual celebration of the Christian Pentecost is found in the legendary *Acts of Paul* which circulated in the second century. There it was said that the Roman governor of Ephesus ordered the apostle to be thrown to the lions 'at the season when Christians did not mourn or bend their knees'. This confirms that the seven weeks of Pentecost, for Jews a time of harvest rejoicing, for Christians represented a succession of Sundays when, as was customary in those days, kneeling, a sign of penitence, was forbidden. The faithful stood to pray, arms upraised to symbolize the resurrection, like the departed souls depicted on the walls of the catacombs. This posture was decreed in Canon 20 of the Council of Nicaea (325) which imposed uniformity of practice, ordering that 'on the Lord's Day and in the days of Pentecost . . . all should at those times offer up their prayers to God standing'. Tertullian (*c*.160–*c*.225), the North African apologist, consoled converts who hankered after pagan festivals by asserting that the pleasure which those celebrations afforded did not equal the joy of the pentecostal season.

Christ revealed

Origen (*c*.185–254), the prolific Alexandrian theologian, in his defence of Christians from attacks made sixty years before by Celsus, an influential Greek philosopher, acknowledged that, although they refused to participate in public festivities, Christians observed four special occasions: the Lord's Day; Preparation Day (the day before the sabbath); Passover (Easter); and Pentecost. A notable omission from this list of events, all connected with Jesus' death and resurrection, is the commemoration of his birth. A possible explanation is that at that time neither pagans nor Christians paid much attention to birthdays as such. For the former, *dies natalis*: (literally) 'birthday', meant the anniversary of the genius, the attendant spirit and divine guardian of an emperor, a city or a temple; for the latter it was the annual remembrance of a martyr's death, the day of rebirth into heaven.

Another possibility is that, in the absence of precise information in the Gospels as to the season when Jesus was born, the word was given a theological meaning. (Shepherds would not have been in the fields 'in the bleak mid-winter', as sung in Christina Rosetti's familiar hymn.) As Justin explained to Trypho, 'a Hebrew of the circumcision' who had escaped to Ephesus after Hadrian's destruction of Jerusalem in 134, Jesus' birth 'really began for men when they first realized who he was'. This happened at his baptism when a voice from heaven was heard to proclaim, 'You are my son;

today have I fathered you' (Lk 3:22), a quotation from the second psalm (Ps 2:7) and a variant reading in early manuscripts for, 'this is my son, the Beloved, my favour rests on him' (Mt 3:17). Christ's baptism was therefore his epiphany (Greek *epiphaneia*: 'manifestation'), when he was revealed to the world as the Son of God, 'my chosen one in whom my soul delights' (Is 42:1).

Evidence that in the fourth century there was an Epiphany festival connected with the commemoration of Jesus' baptism is found in the so-called *Canons of St Athanasius*, a document which, even if it is not by him, is now accepted as belonging to his lifetime (*c.*296–373). Bishops were admonished to give alms to widows and orphans on 'the great festival of the Lord' (Pentecost), 'because on that day the Holy Spirit came down upon the Church'; and 'at the feast of the Lord's Epiphany . . . that is Baptism'. Also mentioned as taking place in the same month, Tybi, the equivalent of January, is another manifestation which happened at the wedding feast at Cana in Galilee when 'our Saviour appeared as God when, by a wonderful miracle, he made the water wine'. Confirmation that the festival was by then widely observed comes from Ammianus Marcellinus, an army officer from Antioch, who noted in his history of the reign of Julian the Apostate (361–63) that the emperor, who had secretly renounced the Christian religion, found it politic at Vienne, in Gaul, to attend church 'on the holy day which Christians celebrate in January and called Epiphany'.

Epiphany was also observed in Spain at this period. In 380 a decree of the Council of Zaragoza ordered that 'for twenty-one days from the sixteenth Kalends of January (17 December) until Epiphany which is the eighth of the Ides of January (6 January), day by day it shall not be permitted that anyone shall be absent from church'. The intention was to prevent the faithful from participating in the revels of the Saturnalia which began on 17 December, 'the merriest time of the year', according to the Latin poet, Catullus. Originally they lasted for seven days but by the fourth century they were often prolonged to include New Year festivities which extended almost until 6 January.

Why that date was chosen for the solemnization of the festival of Christ's revelation has caused much speculation. It was not the date in Alexandria of the winter solstice. The ancient Egyptian solar calendar, reformed by Canopus in 233 BC, in which the year began with the appearance of Sirius, the star which presaged the flooding of the Nile, was coordinated there *c.*26 with the Julian calendar, in which the winter solstice fell on 25 December (actually 21 December). Nor was it a significant date in the ancient Roman world, although an unsupported reference in the *History against the Pagans* (417) by Paulus Orosius claimed that Octavian was hailed as Augustus on 6 January 29 BC when he closed the gates of the Temple of Janus and thus inaugurated a period of peace. Admittedly Augustus was thought to have been divinely appointed to provide the right circumstances for the coming of Christ, but it is unlikely that the date of his triple triumph was in any way connected with Epiphany, a much later development.

What is evident is that by the fourth century Justin's assertion that Jesus' birth for men was 'the time when the knowledge of him was to go forth', i.e., at his baptism, the primary content of Epiphany, was also interpreted in the sense of his physical birth, leading to the celebration of the two events on the same day. Thus St Epiphanius (c 315–403), bishop of Salamis in Cyprus, asserted in his *Panarion*, or 'Medicine Chest', with specifics 'against as many heresies as the number of King Solomon's concubines', that 'Christ was born on the Ides of January, thirteen days after the winter solstice'.

This conflation of the two events in one festival in the East was based on the assumption that the date of Jesus' death was also that of his conception. Some Quartodecimans and other sectaries, possibly those who followed Montanus, an apocalyptic prophet active in Phrygia, maintained that 14 Nisan, the date of the crucifixion, fell on the first full moon of the first Jewish month, thirteen days after 24 March, i.e., 6 April, which was also the day of the incarnation, when Mary said, 'Behold the handmaid of the Lord'. Jesus was therefore born nine months later on 6 January and baptized on the same day when he was thirty years old (Lk 3:23).

Although this date was arrived at by a symbolic method which now appears fanciful, it provides a better explanation for Epiphany than the assertion that the festival was established to counter heretical or pagan celebrations held on the same day. Certainly, in his *Miscellanies* Clement of Alexandria (c.150–215) censured the followers of Basilides (a second-century theologian who taught that Jesus was a man upon whom Christ descended at his baptism) because they celebrated the event 'on the fifteenth or eleventh of the month Tybi' (i.e., 10 or 6 January), but he was attacking an aberration.

In the same way, Epiphanius was describing a pagan custom, not explaining a Christian response, when he noted that on the evening of 5 January the image of the goddess Kôre was carried in procession in Alexandria to the chant, 'Today at this hour Kôre gave birth to the eternal'.

Nor should it be assumed that when Epiphanius noted that a spring at Cibyra and another at Gerasa flowed with wine at the very hour when Jesus performed his first miracle, he was giving the reason why the marriage feast of Cana was eventually associated with Epiphany.

The Armenian Church, which separated from the main Churches in 374, includes the Nativity within its Epiphany festival, which lasts from 5 to 13 January, because Jesus was revealed to all mankind at his baptism whereas at his birth he was made known only to a few. When Epiphany was adopted in regions in the West, notably in Gaul and Spain, as in Orthodox Churches where it ranks next to Easter and Pentecost, it was primarily the theophany, or manifestation of Christ's glory, at his baptism. To this were added other manifestations of his glory: to the Wise Men; and also at Cana in Galilee. St Ambrose (*c*.339–97), bishop of Milan, and the Spanish poet Prudentius (348–*c*.410) praised these theophanies in their hymns, further evidence of their liturgical importance.

Meanwhile, as it will be seen, the birth aspect of Epiphany conflicted in the West with another symbolic date for the Nativity as a physical event, also deduced from the coincidence of conception and death but based on a different premise. It is nevertheless of interest that the date of Easter in a particular year, decided by observations made in Alexandria, a city renowned for its astronomers, and conveyed in so-called 'festal letters', was announced in Rome on 6 January which was also the day when candidates for instruction and eventual baptism at the festival were required to give in their names. This solemn proclamation is still made, or chanted, in a few churches and monasteries.

Christ, 'the true Sun'

Preaching at Antioch *c*.386, John, then a priest and later patriarch of Constantinople, whose eloquence earned him the name of Chrysostom: 'golden-mouthed', said that although opposed by the conservatives in the congregation who clung to Epiphany, for at least ten years many had observed 25 December as the festival of the nativity of Christ. That this was the correct date, he said, was proved by its miraculous and rapid acceptance from Thrace to Cadiz. This date had been arrived at by the method then resorted to, when there was no factual evidence, of allegorical interpretation of scriptural texts. Christ was 'the rising sun from on high', heralded in Zechariah's canticle (Lk 1:78). As foretold by the prophet, probably Ezra, but known as Malachi, 'my messenger', he was 'the sun of justice who would rise with healing in his rays' (Ml 4:2). On a third-century mosaic on a wall of St Peter's necropolis in Rome, he was depicted as Helios, the sun-god, driving his chariot into the heavens. Christ, like the sun, is 'the light of the world' (Jn 8:12). When he became man, he represented a new creation, recalling the first creation, when God said, 'Let there be light' (Gn 1:3). This happened when he divided light from darkness, presumably into equal parts, hence at the vernal equinox, 25 March in the Julian calendar, when day and night are of equal length. He was therefore born nine months later, on 25 December, the winter solstice.

This solar symbolism provided the Christian answer to the worship of *Sol invictus*, a cult encouraged by the emperor Elagabalus (218–22). In decline after his assassination, it was re-established by Aurelian (270–75), who built the temple of Sol: 'the Sun', on the Campus Agrippae in Rome, dedicated on 25 December and thereafter styled *natalis solis invicti*: 'anniversary of the unconquered Sun'. For Christians this was the date of the birth of Christ, 'the true Sun', confirmed by the statement in the *Book of James*, which incorporated traditions current in the second century, that the angel appeared to Zechariah when, as High Priest, 'he took the vestment with twelve bells and went into the Holy of Holies to pray on the Day of Atonement', 23 September. John the Baptist was born on 24 June (now his feast day) and his mother was consequently in the sixth month of her pregnancy on 25 March when the Holy Spirit came upon Mary (Lk 1:26). Christ's birth was therefore on 25 December, exactly as the allegorical method had demonstrated.

That this day had achieved special significance early in the fourth century is proved by an entry in the so-called *Chronograph of 354*, a civil and religious calendar which was destroyed by fire but known through a seventeenth-century copy. From internal evidence it is shown to be a revision of an earlier work, composed 335–6, beautifully inscribed and illustrated by Furius Dionysius Filocalus, a Greek calligrapher in the service of St Damascus I (*c*.304–84). The dedication, *Floreas in Deo Valentine*: 'May you prosper in God, O Valentinus', indicated that it was a New Year present to a wealthy Roman man of affairs who was also a Christian. It lists Roman prefects, pagan festivals, bishops of Rome and anniversaries of burials of Christian martyrs, heading the list of which, suggesting that it then represented the beginning of the Christian year, was the entry, *viii Kal Janu natus Christus in Bethleem Iudeae*: 'On the eighth Kalends of January (25 December) Christ was born in Bethlehem of Judaea.'

The year of Jesus' birth

There existed a tradition, affirmed by Tertullian, that Jewish archives had been removed to Rome by the Emperor Titus (79–81) after he sacked Jerusalem (August 70) and that these contained records of the life and death of Jesus, including the census at the time of his birth. These documents had never come to light, although John of Nikiu (c.900) said that Pope Julius I (337–52), in his attempt to convert the Armenians to 25 December, sent a letter, an obvious forgery, to St Cyril (c.315–86), bishop of Jerusalem, revealing that that was the date registered in the archives.

Contradictory accounts were given in the Gospels of *Matthew* and *Luke*. The former stated that Jesus was born 'in the days of Herod the King', who died c.4 BC, whereas the latter said that it was 'when Cyrenius (Quirinius) was governor of Syria', but his period of office was probably 26–36. The anomaly that Jesus was born BC is attributable to Dionysius Exiguus, who in 533 suggested that *Anno Domini*, 'year of the Lord', should replace the Roman system of counting from the supposed foundation of Rome (AUC). He co-ordinated 754 AUC with 1 AD, but Herod died c.750. According to Luke, 'on the fifteenth year of the reign of Tiberius Caesar [i.e. 27–28] Jesus himself began to be about thirty years of age' (Lk 3:1); this would place his date of birth c.2 BC, according to Dionysius' erroneous computation. Modern chronology favours 7–6(?) BC.

Summary

In the course of a sermon preached at Antioch c.386, St John Chrysostom explained the logical sequence of the four great yearly festivals which had been established by the fourth century. He said: 'If Christ had not been born into the flesh, he would not have been baptized, which is the Theophany; he would not have been crucified and risen, which is the Pascha; he would not have sent down the Spirit, which is Pentecost.' These christological commemorations are the nodal points of the temporale, the section of a Missal or Breviary which sets out the variable parts of the Mass or Office, as distinct from the sanctorale, the part dealing with the festivals of the saints. They comprise two annual cycles: Christmas–Epiphany, at fixed dates in the solar calendar; and Easter–Pentecost, variable because lunar. Around them there developed a complex pattern of observances, derived in part from an interest in the historical, as well as in the theological, implications of the incarnation of God in Christ.

Inevitably this process was observable at an early date in Jerusalem where, under the direction of the Emperor Constantine, and promoted by Cyril, bishop from 349–86, churches were built on sites identified with the life and death of Christ. Services held there, appropriate to the place and the event, and, in many cases, the dramatic re-enactment of the relevant Gospel narrative, stressed the importance of each day as a separate entity. Thus, for example, the Pasch, a unitary festival, was divided into a Good Friday–Easter Sunday observance. In the same way a service held forty days after Easter at the Imbomon, the hillock on the Mount of Olives where Christ was taken up into Heaven and where his footprints were to be seen on the rock, led to the separation of the festival of the Ascension from Pentecost. (In this case an important doctrinal, as well as an historical point was made against the gnostic heresy that Christ was not truly man but a spirit: ghosts do not leave the imprint of their feet!)

Relics from sites in the Holy Land were enshrined in churches in Constantinople, establishing relevant festivals there and encouraging their spread to other parts of the Byzantine Empire. At the same time there were indigenous developments elsewhere, in all probability influenced by the course of readings from the New Testament. Preparation of candidates for baptism also complicated the calendar, causing an extended season of self-denial and emphasis on particular Sundays, for example the Delivery of the Creed (*Traditio symboli*) on Palm Sunday. These are but a few early instances of the origins of modern seasonal and festal observances which are discussed in the sections which follow.

The Week

Sunday

EVELYN UNDERHILL (1875–1941), THE ENGLISH writer on the mystical life, defined worship as 'the response of the creature to the Eternal'. This response may be expressed through personal devotions, performed at whatever time, or in whatever place, an individual chooses. 'One is nearer God's Heart in a garden/Than anywhere else on earth', may be true for Dorothy Frances Gurney (1858–1932), and for those who have the gift of self-discipline and private prayer, but it is nevertheless the Christian tradition that solitary devotion is part of, and dependent upon, regular worship with the rest of the Christian community. The principal day for this assembly is Sunday, the Lord's Day, when the faithful gather together in the Lord's house (which by way of medieval Greek becomes 'church' in English and 'kirk' in lowland Scots).

In his encyclical *Mediator Dei* (1947), Pius XII described communal worship as instituted for 'the glory of God and the sanctification and education of the faithful', a definition acceptable to Christians of all denominations, but each one may differ as to form and content. This is perceptible in the architectural setting, the interior arrangement and furnishings of the building in which they meet. Where worship is primarily sacramental, centred on the celebration of Mass, Eucharist, or Holy Communion, whichever term is preferred, the focal point is the altar. Where the emphasis is on the exposition of scripture, and the Lord's Supper less frequent, an elevated rostrum, or pulpit, may stand centrally, with a table in front, or prominently but to one side so as not to obscure the altar. Quakers, a non-sacramental association, sit facing each other in a plain meeting-house, waiting for the spirit to move them to read, speak or pray.

John XXIII's policy of *aggiornamento*: 'bringing the Church up to date', implemented by the Second Vatican Council (1962–65) and matched by similar movements for liturgical reform in other Churches, profoundly affected all aspects of communal worship. As expressed in the *Constitution of the Liturgy* (1969) this involves the whole people of God, priest and laity, each according to his special role. At Mass, the president (literally 'one who sits facing') now performs the manual acts and says the words of consecration from behind the altar, in close proximity to the congregation, thus stressing their unity. This necessitated the reordering of churches built according to the medieval plan in which Mass was celebrated by the priest who faced the altar in the sanctuary at the east end, remote from worshippers standing or sitting in the elongated nave.

A fundamental reform was the substitution for the Latin of the Tridentine Mass, formulated by the Council of Trent (1545–63), of the revised vernacular Mass, authorized in 1970 in the new *Roman Missal*, the change from ecclesiastical language to the national tongue anticipated by Thomas Cranmer who promoted *The Booke of the common prayer* (1549). By 'common' was meant that services should be shared, said 'in common' in language 'understanded of the people', a principle which was maintained in the *Book of Common Prayer*, the standard for worship in the Church of England and the only book authorized by Parliament. The 'Prayer Book (alternative and other services) Measure (1966)' permitted experimentation, to take into account new theological insights, linguistic change and modern social needs, a process which culminated in the *Alternative Service Book* (1980), sanctioned for use by the General Synod. Similar revisions were undertaken in the Episcopal Church of the USA (1979) and in other Churches in the Anglican Communion.

Sunday has thus been restored to the pre-eminence which it held in the early Church, taking precedence over all other feasts and festivals. Central to Christian worship, it is the joyful celebration of salvation promised through Christ's death and resurrection and a foretaste of the eternal bliss which awaits all true believers.

Morning and Evening Prayer

St Benedict of Nursia's *Rule*, the code of discipline for conventual life, composed c.540, created the pattern for *opus dei*: 'the service of God', the round of private devotions, prayer, study and work observed by most monastic communities. It was structured around the recitation in the choir, at the east end of the church, of the Divine Office, prayers, psalms, antiphons and readings, said or sung at fixed hours of the day according to the Roman system which divided the twelve hours from sunrise to sunset into four watches, the sixth hour falling at midday: Prime ('first', 6 a.m.), Terce ('third', 9 a.m.), Sext ('sixth', at noon), and None ('ninth', 3 p.m.). To conform to the words of the psalm, 'Seven times a day I praise you', and 'At midnight I rise to praise you' (Ps 119/118:164,62), there were added Lauds (Latin *laudes*: 'praises') in the early morning, Vespers ('evening prayer') and Compline ('completion', before retiring for the night). St Benedict also prescribed Matins (English Mattins), a night office at 2 a.m. (called Vigils until the eleventh century), but it became the practice to anticipate it, saying the office the evening before.

The day Hours recalled incidents in the Passion ('suffering') of Christ:

> *At Mattins bound, at Prime reviled,*
> *condemned to death at Terce,*
> *Nailed to the Cross at Sext, at None*
> *his blessed side they pierce.*
> *They take him down at Vesper-tide,*
> *in grave at Compline lay,*
> *Who henceforth bids his Church observe*
> *her sevenfold Hours alway.*

When he was a monk, Martin Luther (1483–1546) found these Hours onerous and, once free from his monastic vows, proposed that they should be reduced to two, Morning and Evening Prayer, a reform which became effective in the German Lutheran Church. Probably inspired by Luther's example, Thomas Cranmer, who was in Nuremberg the year before he became archbishop of Canterbury in 1533, to encourage attendance at church, included only two daily services, Mattins and Evensong, in *The Booke of the common prayer* (1549). In contrast to the often inaudible Hours in Latin, these were ordered to be said by the minister, 'standing and turning him so as he may beste be heard of all such as be present'. It was further provided that, 'in such places as they doe sing, there shall the lessons be songe in a playne tune after the manner of distincte reading'. This was achieved a year later when John Merbecke, organist of St George's Chapel, Windsor, published *The Booke of Common Praier Noted*, that is, set to a melodic, yet simple, plainchant.

In the Preface to *The Booke of common praier* (1559), the Elizabethan prayer book used by William Shakespeare and John Donne, it was ordered that 'the curate [the parochial minister who had the 'cure', or care of souls], being at home and not being otherwise letted [hindered],' shall say Morning and Evening Prayer 'daily in the parish church or chapel . . . and shall toll a bell . . . that such as be disposed may come to hear God's word and pray with him'. The printers of *The Temple*, the collected poems of the saintly George

Herbert (1593–1633), priest at Bemerton, near Salisbury, wrote that he honoured this obligation so punctiliously that he 'drew the greater part of his parishioners to accompanie him dayly in the publick celebration of Divine Service'.

This could not be said of many parishes, then or now, although Anglican clergy, who may fulfil this duty in various ways, are theoretically still required to say Morning and Evening prayer daily in the church in which they minister. (Shorter alternatives are now provided to encourage lay attendance.) On Sundays, however, these two services, with Holy Communion following Mattins (Morning Prayer) according to the *Book of Common Prayer*, as authorized by Parliament in 1662, became the forms of worship most in vogue in England and the colonies. Revised according to need, these services formed the basis of the prayer books of the various Churches in the Anglican Communion.

Hymns, many composed by reputable poets, or translated from the sacred songs of the early Church; psalms in Miles Coverdale's versions (1535) from the Vulgate Bible; and readings at these services from the so-called King James' Bible, 'appointed' (not 'authorized') in 1611, became part of the English musical and literary heritage. Choral settings of the *Magnificat*: 'My soul doth magnify the Lord', the Blessed Virgin's song of praise, and of the *Nunc dimittis*: 'Lord, now lettest thou thy servant depart in peace', Simeon's canticle when he beheld the Christ child, are in the best tradition of English cathedral music.

The Liturgy of the Hours

In the Roman Catholic Church, the *Breviary*, the liturgical book containing the Divine Office, had become almost unmanageable by the sixteenth century as a result of the multiplication of saints' days, each with its 'proper' ('suitable to the day') material. Cardinal Francisco de Quiñones (*d.*1540), who to some degree influenced Thomas Cranmer's liturgical reforms, produced a simplified version, known by the name of his titular church in Rome as the *Breviary of the Holy Cross*. Approved by Paul III (1534–39), it was widely used until proscribed by Paul IV in 1558. A new *Breviary* was published in the wake of reforms advocated by the Council of Trent (1545–63) and continued as the official book until 1971, when, promoted by the Second Vatican Council, a new *Liturgy of the Hours: The Divine Office* was substituted.

According to the 'General Instruction', this was 'so devised that the whole course of the day and night is made holy by the praise of God'. The office of Prime was omitted but 'those who have received the mandate to celebrate the Liturgy of the Hours', namely bishops, priests, other sacred ministers and those under religious obedience, are required 'to recite the whole sequence of Hours each day'. Unless for serious reasons, Lauds, as Morning Prayer, and Vespers, Evening Prayer, are never to be omitted. This last regulation is important because it makes possible, as was the purpose of the reform, the attendance at daily prayer 'of all the people of God', clerical and lay, the hope being that the latter may be present, either on their way to or from work, at one or other of these principal Hours, or at least at Compline at the end of the day.

The Seasons

Advent

ALTHOUGH, AS IN ANCIENT TIMES, 25 DECEMBER, the solemnity of the Nativity of Our Lord, may be regarded as the beginning of the Christian year, the annual liturgical cycle starts on Advent Sunday, the Sunday nearest to, or on, St Andrew's Day, 30 November, the earliest date being 27 November and the latest 3 December. There follows a season of spiritual preparation for Christmas, the English name for the festival, derived from *cristes-messe*: '(Festival) Mass of Christ'. The season ends at the first prayer on Christmas Eve, 24 December.

Within this period are four Sundays, either numbered consecutively, First, Second, Third and Fourth 'of' (or 'in') Advent, or inversely, Fourth, Third, Second and Next 'before Christmas'.

In the Roman empire, the accession of an emperor, accorded divine honours since the time of Augustus (68 BC–14 AD), and the ceremonial entry of a ruler to a province or a city, were his 'advent' (Latin *adventus*: 'arrival'). The obverse of a gold medallion found at Arras depicts the advent in 296 of Constantius Chlorus at the gates of the city of London. Constantine the Great, his son, was shown on his triumphal arch being welcomed into Rome after his victory at the Milvian Bridge on 29 October 312, a date recorded in the *Chronograph of 354* as *adventus divi*: 'coming of the deified one'. Latin-speaking Christians, for whom Jesus Christ was the only true Lord and Emperor, borrowed the word and the concept but invested it with a new meaning: 'the coming of their Saviour'.

Sermons like those 'On the Advent of Christ' preached by St Maximus (*d.*408/23), bishop of Turin, indicate that Advent was originally the festival day itself. Later the same word was used for the weeks leading up to it, a Western innovation seemingly originating in the monastic practice of observing a strict regime before major festivals. Irish Penitentials, books containing directions for confessors, reveal that Christmas, ranking with

29

Easter and Pentecost, was preceded by the first of three named fasts, the fast of Elijah, recalling his forty-days and forty-nights journey through the wilderness to Mount Horeb (IK 19:8). The Venerable Bede recorded that in Northumbria Bishop Eadbert (*d.*698) was accustomed to spend 'forty days before the Nativity of Our Lord in prayer, penitence and fasting'. St Egbert (*d.*729), who had studied in Ireland and later became abbot of the monastic community at Iona, for forty days before Christmas, 'as during Lent', existed on a scanty ration of bread and skimmed milk.

In Gaul, St Gregory (*c.*540–94), bishop of Tours, noted that Perpetuus, his fifth-century predecessor, had ordered fasting on three days, Mondays, Wednesdays and Fridays, 'from the burial of St Martin until the feast of the Nativity'. The first Council of Mâcon (582) imposed this duty on the entire province, religious, clergy and laity alike, and ordered that Mass should be celebrated 'according to the quadragesimal (Lenten) rite'. This is the origin of St Martin's Lent which follows Martinmas, the date of his burial on 11 November, one of his two feast days, the other being 4 July, the anniversary of his consecration as bishop and of the translation of his relics to the new church dedicated to him in Tours. Martinmas, the traditional time for slaughtering pigs and salting the meat for winter provisions, thus acquired the festive character of Shrove Tuesday, the carnival before the austerities of Lent.

In Rome, except for 'the feast of the tenth month' in December, so called because in the time of St Leo the Great (440–61) the year began in March, it would seem that the period before Christmas was characterized by joyful expectancy, white vestments being worn at Mass. Charlemagne (*c.*742–814) adopted the Roman rite for use in his imperial chapel at Aachen (Aix-la-Chapelle) but, as the rite was accepted throughout his realms in the ninth century, Advent acquired the austerity associated with Gallican monastic practice, although discipline was not so severe as in Lent and many sought dispensation from fasting. In 1362, Urban V, who even after his election continued to live as a Benedictine monk, was compelled to insist that the papal court should set a good example of Advent abstinence!

Although the concept of forty days of self-denial influenced the duration of the Advent season, the number of Sundays to be included varied according to province. From the so-called *Bobbio Missal*, a liturgical manuscript found in an Italian town of that name near Genoa, it may be deduced that in the eighth century in Gaul three Sundays were normal in some churches, whereas in the Ambrosian rite, traditionally attributed to St Ambrose (*c.*339–97), bishop of Milan, the season encompassed six Sundays, as it does today in that diocese. Amalarius of Metz (c.780–850), the liturgical scholar, attributed the reduction to four Sundays to St Gregory the Great (590–604) who preached Advent sermons on these Sundays in the basilica of Santa Maria Maggiore, which by then had become the focus of Christmas observance in Rome.

In keeping with the solemnity of the Advent season, seen as the time when the people 'walked in darkness' (Is 9:2), many churches present a somewhat austere appearance. Except on saints' days, the predominant liturgical colour is purple; there is an absence of flowers; and the organ is usually played only to accompany choral and congregational singing. Omitted from the Divine Office is the hymn *Te Deum laudamus*: 'We praise thee, O God'. So that the *Gloria in excelsis Deo*: 'Glory to God in the highest', the angelic hymn which greeted the birth of Jesus, may resound with greater significance at Christmas, it is not sung at Mass. The nuptial blessing, forbidden at this season by the Council of Trent, is now given, but couples intending to be married are asked to keep in mind the meaning of Advent.

An apparently anomalous intrusion into the mood of quiet contemplation may occur on the third Sunday, once called *Gaudete* Sunday after the Latin word which began the introit, 'Rejoice in the Lord always'. Rose-coloured vestments are permitted, the organ is played and the sanctuary may be decorated with flowers. This is usually explained as the survival of the medieval custom, modelled on mid-Lent Sunday, of providing a respite from abstinence. In fact, it may have originated at an earlier period when, following the Roman custom of nominating consuls and magistrates around 17 December, the Church ordained priests and deacons on the evening of the fourth Sunday, which was therefore 'vacant', without a Mass. The third Sunday was thus the last effective corporate eucharistic gathering before Christmas and, as was then the custom, it was a joyful day.

On each of the four Sundays, candles in an Advent wreath, a circle of evergreen foliage, may be lighted consecutively to symbolize the approach of the light 'which shines in darkness' (Jn 1:5), a custom which originated in Germany in the nineteenth century. An Advent Star, a model lighted from within, first made around 1850 for the Moravian Brethren in East Germany, recalls 'the bright star of the morning' (Rv 22:16) and the star which led the Wise Men to Bethlehem. At pre-Christmas services children hold a decorated orange in which is inserted a small candle, also of Moravian origin and called Christingle, possibly the anglicization of the German *Christ-*

kindl: 'Christ-child', or *Christ-engel*: 'Christ-angel', the angel who gives gifts to children.

'It was foretold', Justin explained to Trypho the Jew, 'that there would be two advents of Christ: one in which he will appear in suffering and without honour or beauty; the second in which he will return in glory to judge all men.' The first advent happened when Jesus was born in humble circumstances in Bethlehem. As prophesied by Isaiah, salvation would come through 'a man of sorrows, and acquainted with grief', one who 'hath no form nor comeliness: and when we shall see him, there is no beauty that we should desire him' (Is 53:2), a description not favoured in art but realized so effectively in the paintings of Georges Rouault (1871–1958) and, in sculpture, by Jacob Epstein (1880–1959). The other advent, 'the second coming' (Justin was the first to use this phrase), will be when Christ will return as judge of the world, possibly on the anniversary of his birth.

Over the centuries, Advent has therefore had a dual significance: it looks forward to the celebration of Christ's coming in the flesh, and it prepares the faithful for the end-time when all will be summoned to appear before the judgment seat. It is no coincidence that *Dies irae*: 'day of wrath', a poem intended as an aid to private devotion, ascribed to Thomas of Celano, biographer of St Francis of Assisi, was adopted as a sequence, or verses sung before the gospel, for the Sunday before Advent. The terrors of this day were vividly displayed in sculptured tympana and stained glass windows on the west front of churches, the point of the setting sun, symbolic of the end of time. On the chancel arch a 'doom' (from the Old English for 'sentencing'), in direct view of the congregation, was a reminder that to enter heaven (symbolized by the sanctuary) all must suffer judgment.

Although modern Advent lectionaries describe the terrifying moment when 'the day of the Lord will come as a thief in the night, in which the heavens shall pass away with a great noise, and the elements shall melt with fervent heat' (2P 3:10), and although it is certain that each individual will be required to account for lifetime actions, the emphasis is now less on the separation of the sheep from the goats, or the burning of the chaff on the winnowing floor, and more on Christ's mercy because, as Isaiah prophesied, 'he will judge with integrity'. Meanwhile the faithful are urged to continue their good works, welcoming the stranger, clothing those in need, feeding the hungry, visiting the sick and those in prison (Mt 25:31–46), so that, as expressed in the Advent collect composed by Thomas Cranmer, 'when he shall come again in his glorious Majesty to judge both the quick ('the living') and the dead, we may rise to life immortal'.

An early-third-century fresco in the catacomb of Priscilla in Rome depicts a Roman matron with a child on her lap, possibly one of the earliest representations of Mary as Mother of God. Slightly to the left, an old man, undoubtedly Balaam, 'the man with far-seeing eyes', points upwards to a star discernible on the rough wall, recalling his words, 'there shall come a Star out of Jacob, and a Sceptre shall rise out of Israel' (Nb 24:17), one of the prophecies incorporated in the readings for Advent from the prophets of the old dispensation, foremost among whom was Isaiah. He looked forward to the coming of the ruler who would inaugurate the Messianic age when the peoples of the world 'shall beat their swords into ploughshares, and their spears into pruninghooks: nation shall not lift up sword against nation, neither shall they learn war any more' (Is 2:4), part of which text is inscribed on a wall facing the entrance to the United Nations building in New York.

Isaiah said that this era of peaceful co-existence would be heralded when 'there shall come forth a rod out of the stem of Jesse, and a Branch shall grow out of his roots' (Is II:1). This is the source of the many depictions of the ancestors of Christ in which Jesse, the father of David, Shepherd-King of Israel, whose royal city was Bethlehem, is shown as an old man, a lantern alongside him indicating that he is asleep and dreaming. From his loins grows a tree on which appear Jesus' forebears, either selected from the symbolic fourteen generations beginning with Abraham (Mt 1:1–17), or reaching back to Adam (Lk 3:23–38), signifying that Christ is the Second Adam who has come to save all mankind.

The most important, and controversial, of Isaiah's Advent texts is, 'Behold, a virgin shall conceive, and bear a son, and shall call his name Immanuel' (Is 7:14), which, as the writer of the *Gospel of Matthew* explained, 'being interpreted is, God with us' (Mt I:23). As Trypho told Justin, and many have done so since in the debate over Jesus' virginal conception (*not* 'virgin birth', the popular phrase), '*almah*, the word in the original Hebrew, rendered into Greek as *parthenos*: 'virgin', meant a young girl of marriageable age, or a newly-wed woman, without specific reference to her virginal state. Nevertheless, Isaiah intended a special event, using this word instead of *betula*: 'virgin', when he reassured King Ahaz (*c.*734 BC) of Judah that his realm would be free from Assyrian invaders when a certain young woman gave birth to a son whom she would call Immanuel, sign of God's protection. Christians understood this prophecy to refer not only to a

33

particular historical event but also to the moment in the future when God would send his son to redeem the world. As St Thomas Aquinas explained, 'In order that Christ's body might be shown to be a real body, he was born of a woman: in order that his Godhead might be made clear, he was born of a virgin.'

Appropriate to this theme are the Advent lections recalling the annunciation to Mary, liturgically celebrated on 25 March, and the appearance in a dream of an angel, traditionally Gabriel, to Joseph, betrothed to Mary who, before they set up house together, discovered that she was pregnant. A just man, unwilling to expose her to public ridicule, or death by stoning, the punishment for adultery, he resolved to divorce her privately in the presence of two witnesses, the minimum legal requirement. The angel assured him that 'that which is conceived in her is of the Holy Spirit', and ordered that Joseph should call the child Jesus (from the Hebrew *Jehoshua*: 'God saves') 'because he will save his people from their sins' (Mt I:18–21).

In ancient Rome, 17 December marked the beginning of the Saturnalia, revels in honour of the god Saturnus which originally lasted for seven days and coincided with the week leading up to Christmas. As an alternative to these often licentious festivities, Christians were offered even greater opportunities for preparing themselves for the coming of Christ. The last week of Advent is therefore a time of renewed devotional activity, each day with its 'proper' (appointed for the day) Mass.

A special, and impressive, feature of this week is the singing at Evening Prayer of the Great Advent Antiphons, known as the Seven O's because each one begins with an invocation of Christ, using one of his divine names: Wisdom, Lord, Root of Jesse, Key of David, Day-spring, King of Nations, and Emmanuel. Of unknown authorship, these antiphons, adding up to the number which symbolizes perfection, were composed before the ninth century when they were referred to by Amalarius of Metz.

In the Sarum calendar, used in Salisbury cathedral, an anthem in honour of St Mary the Virgin, *O Virgo virginum*: 'O Virgin of virgins', was sung at Vespers on 23 December. The O antiphons therefore began on 16 December, a date retained as *O Sapientia*: 'O Wisdom', in the *Book of Common Prayer*.

Christmastide

'The Nativity of our Lord, or the Birthday of Christ commonly called Christmas Day' is the all-embracing title in the *Book of Common Prayer* for the solemnity which is second in importance to Easter. Like Easter it is one of the two days in the year which has an octave, eight days during which the festival continues to be observed. Unlike Easter, the date of which varies, Christmas is fixed in the calendar and falls on the same date within the traditional Twelve Days of Christmas, a time of celebration which begins at the first evening prayer on Christmas Eve, 24 December, and includes Twelfth Night, the evening preceding 6 January, the Epiphany of the Lord.

CHRISTMAS EVE Christmas is one of three festivals, the others being Easter and Pentecost, before which there is a solemn vigil, a nocturnal service of prayer. This may be followed by the Vigil Mass which looks forward to the great day which is about to dawn. God told Moses that he would send the starving Israelites 'bread from heaven', interpreted as foreshadowing the eucharistic body of Christ, 'the bread of life' (Jn 6:35). St Jerome (c.342–420), the Venerable Bede and many others have perceived divine providence in the fact that Jesus was born in Bethlehem, a place-name of uncertain etymology but assumed by them to mean 'house of bread'. Moses promised the Israelites that in the morning they would see 'the glory of the Lord' (Ex 16:17), the splendour of God's presence, a phrase echoed in the communion antiphon, 'the glory of the Lord will be revealed' (Is 40:5), a fitting prelude to the great day which is about to dawn.

At this Mass, 'Glory to God in the highest', the angelic hymn, is once again proclaimed. It is customary to kneel when the words, 'and was incarnate of the Holy Spirit and was made man' are said in the Creed.

A crib, or creche, a model of the 'lowly cattle shed', as in the carol, in which stands a cradle surrounded by figurines of Mary, Joseph and the Shepherds, to which three Kings are added at Epiphany, may be placed in many churches at this season. An aid to devotion, it was popularized by the Order of Friars Minor whose founder, St Francis (1181/2–1226), vested as a deacon, sang the gospel as Mass was celebrated at Christmas in 1223 in a stable which he had asked a local landowner, identified as Giovanni da Velliti, to erect in the woods at Greccio, about forty-five miles south of his native city of Assisi. Thomas of Celano, the saint's first official biographer, wrote that Francis wished to bring vividly before his very eyes the hardships suffered by the Christ Child, 'how he lay in a manger on the hay, with the ox and the ass standing by'. As Francis preached, one near him had a vision of a little child of surpassing beauty asleep in the cradle, 'whom St Francis awakened as he embraced him in both arms'.

Although not mentioned in the Gospel narratives of Jesus' birth, at least since the early third century when they were carved on the cover of a Roman sarcophagus, the ox and the ass have been assumed to have been present in the stable. The earliest literary reference to them is an eighth- or ninth-century Latin manuscript, allegedly authenticated by St Jerome as a translation of the (nonexistent) Hebrew original of *The Gospel of Matthew*. There it was stated that Mary 'went into a stable and put her child in a manger, and an ox and an ass worshipped him'. This conflated two messianic prophecies: 'the ox knows his owner and the ass his master's crib' (Is I:3); and 'Between two beasts are you known' (Ha 3:2 in the Septuagint version).

CHRISTMAS DAY   The solemnity of the Nativity of Our Lord is one of two days (the other, albeit for a different reason, being All Souls' Day) on which a priest may preside at three successive Masses: at night, the popular Midnight Mass; at dawn; and during the day. In England, in 1549, two communion services were envisaged, but only the one during the day was eventually retained. Modern Anglican practice is to provide appropriate introductory sentences and alternative readings which permit three eucharistic services where these are customary at Christmas.

Benedict XIV (1740–58), a liturgical scholar, ascribed a spiritual meaning to the three Masses, by his time thought to have been the result of divine providence. They represented, he said: Christ's eternal birth in the bosom of the Father; his birth as man of Mary; and his spiritual birth in the hearts of the faithful. In fact they were not instituted with this intention but originated accidentally in Rome where, at Christmas, in the sixth century, popes held 'stations' (eucharistic assemblies) at three locations. They went at night to the oratory adjoining the basilica of Santa Maria Maggiore which contained a replica of the manger in the Church of the Nativity at Bethlehem. At dawn, to honour the influential Greek community, they processed to the Church of St Anastasia which enshrined some of her relics, brought from Constantinople where her feast day was kept on 25 December (now 21 December in the Orthodox calendar). They then returned to St Peter's for the usual Christmas Mass, although from the eleventh century onwards it became customary to remain at Santa Maria Maggiore for the day Mass celebrated in the chapel containing two wooden panels, believed to have formed part of the manger in which the new-born Christ Child was placed. In the ninth century, when Charlemagne imposed Roman liturgical usage in his imperial domains, the pope's prerogative to preside at three Christmas Masses devolved on three different priests. Permission for one priest to celebrate all three was given in the time of Peter the Venerable (*c.*1092–1156), abbot of the Benedictine monastery at Cluny, France.

At these three Masses, white or gold vestments are worn, expressive of the joy experienced because, as in words made universally familiar by Handel's *Messiah*, 'the people who walked in darkness have seen a great light . . . For unto us a child is given . . . and his name shall be called "Wonderful Counsellor, Mighty God, Everlasting Father, Prince of Peace". . . .' (Is 9:2–6). He is the true light which darkness could not overcome, as celebrated in the sublime hymn, the prologue to the *Gospel of John*. In art this light is shown radiating from the Christ Child, illuminating the features of Mary, Joseph and the Shepherds and penetrating the surrounding darkness.

The conventional location of Jesus' birth in a stable, 'because there was no room for them in the inn', presents certain textual problems. The word translated as 'inn' actually means the large upper room of a house, and 'room' could also mean 'space', so that it may be assumed that, to obtain privacy, Mary withdrew to the ground floor in part of which cattle were stabled. This conflicts with another tradition, current in the second century and incorporated in the *Book of James*, that Mary experienced the onset of birth pangs as she journeyed to Bethlehem and Joseph led her to a cave where she gave birth. Justin, in his dialogue with Trypho the Jew, harmonized these two versions, explaining that when Joseph could not find a place to lodge in the village, he went to a cave nearby 'where Mary brought forth the child and laid him in a manger', which suggests that the cave also sheltered cattle. Justin saw this as the fulfilment of Isaiah's prophecy, 'the craggy rocks will be his refuge' (Is 33:16).

Origen, the Alexandrian theologian, and other third-century pilgrims to the Holy Land, were shown this cave. In the *Life of Constantine*, ascribed to Eusebius, bishop of Caesarea, it was recorded that in 339 Helena, the emperor's mother, 'erected a richly-adorned basilica over the grotto of Christ's nativity'. The Christmas Mass is now celebrated in one of the series of caves beneath the modern Church of the Nativity where a plaque marks the place on which the manger stood. Early Western art, influenced by the Byzantine convention, depicts a cave, or a shelter at the mouth of a cave, but later this yields to the portrayal of a stable with the ox and the ass in attendance. Influenced by boisterous episodes in medieval plays, many paintings show Mary and Joseph seeking refuge in a stable because a disobliging innkeeper has turned them away from his establishment which overflows with travellers who have come to Bethlehem for the census.

THE HOLY FAMILY OF JESUS, MARY AND JOSEPH Although not unknown in the late Middle Ages, devotion to the united Holy Family, an expression of Counter-Reformation piety, achieved widespread popularity from the seventeenth century onwards. St Francis de Sales (1567–1622), co-founder of the Order of the Visitation, wrote that the three persons of the Holy Family were the earthly counterpart of the heavenly Trinity. This concept influenced the composition of the *Two Trinities*, painted in 1670 by Bartolomé Esteban Murillo (1617–88), which is based on the intersection of two triangles, symbols of the Trinity, with Jesus as the nexus between the inverted upper one, containing God the Father and the Holy Spirit, and the ground-based lower one where the lines enclose Mary and Joseph, protector of the divine child.

As the model for the Christian family, the devotion was fostered by the Jesuits and by the Society of Saint-Sulpice, a congregation of secular priests founded in 1642 in the parish of that name in Paris. The cult was encouraged in French-speaking Canada by François de Montmorency Laval (1623–1708), first bishop of Quebec. It was developed in the industrial regions of France and Belgium in the nineteenth century as movements of population threatened the break-up of family life. Fraternities were founded under the patronage of the Holy Family, one of the earliest being formed in Liège in 1844 by Henri Belletable, a retired noncommissioned officer in the Belgian army. Encouraged by Pius IX in 1847 and by Leo XIII in 1892, these pious associations were rewarded in 1921 when Benedict XV instituted the universal feast of the Holy Family, to be kept on the first Sunday after Epiphany. In 1969 this feast was transferred to the first Sunday after Christmas, or to 30 December, if Christmas falls on a Sunday.

Appropriate to the day, although the event happened during the great Passover pilgrimage, is the very human story of Joseph and Mary anxiously returning to Jerusalem to search for Jesus when they could not find him among their neighbours and relations as they made their way home to Nazareth. They discovered him in one of the colonnaded courts of the Temple, addressing the doctors of the Law and astonishing them with his knowledge of the scriptures. Then twelve years old, Jesus was actually a year younger than it was considered fitting for a boy to read from the scroll of the Law, which he was allowed to do publicly at his *bar miswah*, proof that he had attained manhood. There are alternative translations for Mary's relieved, yet reproachful, 'Why have you done this to us? See how worried your father and I have been looking for you!' One version of Jesus' reply reads, 'Did you not know that I must be in my Father's house?' which accords with the location of the incident. The other, 'that I must be about my Father's business', is a statement of his divine mission. That he returned with Joseph and Mary to Nazareth and remained with them until his baptism is proof of mutual love and the stability of the family (Lk 2:41–52).

NAMING OF JESUS   Circumcision, the removal of the foreskin, sign of the Lord God's everlasting covenant with the people of Israel, was performed on a male child on the eighth day after his birth. Jesus, in Paul's words 'born a subject of the Law' (Ga 4:4), was circumcised 'when the eighth day came' (Lk 2:21). No mention is made of the season, but when 25 December was adopted in the West as the commemorative festival of Jesus' birth, the eighth day, the octave, coincided with the Kalends of January, the first day of the Roman year in the calendar reformed in 46 BC by Julius Caesar in his role as *pontifex maximus*: 'chief priest', and the culmination of the Saturnalia. Outraged by the bloody games staged on that day in the Roman stadium, Almacius (or Telemachus), an Eastern monk, c.351 rushed into the arena shouting, 'Cease from the superstition of idols and polluted sacrifices. Today is the octave of the Lord.' He was either stoned to death by infuriated spectators or killed by gladiators on the orders of Alpicius, prefect of the city. His feast day is 1 January.

The problem which faced the Church at this period was to provide Christian alternatives to New Year pagan festivities which then, as now, were a deeply-rooted feature of popular culture. St Augustine of Hippo preached that time spent in church was better than watching indecent mimes, and listening to the music of psalms more profitable than hearing bawdy song. He urged his congregation to give money to the poor instead of exchanging wax candles, dolls and pottery figurines, then the customary New Year's gifts. St Sedatus, bishop of Nîmes in Gaul early in the sixth century, protested against drunken orgies and men dressing up as women, or disguising themselves as wild beasts at this season. The second provincial Council of Tours (567) ordered that for the three days of the Kalends of January, 'following the example of our fathers . . . to tread underfoot the custom of the gentiles', there should be penitential exercises and, 'at the eighth hour (2 p.m.) . . . the Mass of Circumcision, pleasing to God' should be celebrated.

As the Roman rite spread throughout the West from the ninth century onwards, 1 January became a feast day rather than a fast, with emphasis on the event commemorated on the octave day of the Nativity. Following the usage of Sarum, the *Book of Common Prayer* retained the title, 'The Circumcision of Christ'. That the sinless child submitted to the rite which St Augustine of Hippo concluded was the sacred sign of the remedy for original sin, was interpreted as an example of obedience to the Law which he had come, not to abolish, but to fulfil. He took upon himself the yoke of the Law to free mankind from the yoke of the devil, and circumcision, the first shedding of his blood, foreshadowed his sacrificial death. As expressed in the collect for the day in the *Book of Common Prayer*, it was also intended as an example, so that all may be granted 'the true circumcision of the spirit; that our hearts and all our members, being mortified from all worldly and carnal lusts, we may in all things obey thy blessed will'.

At the time of circumcision, like all Jewish male children, Jesus was given his name, as announced to Mary, and to Joseph in a dream, derived from Hebrew *Yehoshua*, Aramaic *Yeshua* or *Yeshu*, meaning 'God helps', popularly interpreted as 'God saves'. For this reason the rite was seen as foretelling the baptismal service when the infant is given its Christian name. Modern Anglican custom is therefore to place less emphasis on the aspect of circumcision and more on the naming of Jesus. In the *Roman Missal* the day is now a solemnity of the Blessed Virgin Mary, Mother of God.

THE EPIPHANY OF THE LORD   The Gospel narrative on which this festival is founded (Mt 2:1–12) has three folkloric elements: a star which presages the birth of a great man; a king who attempts by a ruse to discover the whereabouts of a hidden rival; and the supernatural frustration of the plan to kill the child. In the Greek text the Wise Men who come to Jerusalem enquiring for the new-born king of the Jews are called *magoi*, Latin *magi*: 'magicians', or 'astrologers'. An early-fourth-century painting on an arch in the catacomb of Priscilla in Rome shows them wearing Phrygian caps, full-sleeved belted tunics and trousers, the garb of the priests of Zoroaster, the Persian prophet, who watched the heavens for the appearance of the star which would herald the birth of the saviour-god. Conical caps in other depictions identify them as Jews, possibly descendants of the captives who remained in Babylon, ancient centre of astrological studies, who looked for the star of Balaam's prophecy (Nb 24:17) which would announce the coming of the Messiah. Isaiah had prophesied, 'Kings will be your foster-fathers . . . They will fall prostrate before you . . . (Is

49:23), and in a psalm it was foretold that, 'the Kings of Tarshish and the islands will pay him tribute . . . The Kings of Sheba and Saba will offer gifts' (Ps 72/71:10–11). From these texts it was assumed that the Wise Men were also kings, and it is in the latter guise that they appear in art from the tenth century onwards. They are three in number, to accord with their three gifts, gold, frankincense and myrrh, and the three kingdoms named in the psalm. As it was prophesied that 'the nations will come to your light and kings to your dawning brightness' (Is 60:3), the kings were also understood to represent the three races of mankind, descended from Noah's sons, Ham, Shem and Japheth, and their encounter with the Christ Child, 'the manifestation of Christ to the gentiles', the subtitle for Epiphany added in 1662 to the *Book of Common Prayer*.

Herod's cunning plan to find his potential rival and then to dispose of him was thwarted when the Wise Men were warned in a dream not to go back to Jerusalem. An angel also appeared to Joseph to tell him to take the child and his mother to Egypt because Herod was about to search for Jesus and kill him. The writer of the *Gospel of Matthew* perceived that this was foreseen in the prophecy, 'I called my son out of Egypt' (Ho II:1), in which 'son' in the first instance meant 'Israel', the people of the old dispensation, but Jesus, God's son, in the new. As the Wise Men 'returned to their own country by a different way', they are sometimes shown in medieval art aboard a ship, in contrast to their arrival on horseback.

In the East, 6 January was the festival commemorating Jesus' birth and baptism. To these manifestations of his divinity were added two other revelations of himself: to the Wise Men; and at Cana when he changed water into wine. To avoid a double celebration of the Nativity, 25 December in the West, 6 January in Rome and elsewhere became the festival of his manifestation to the Three Kings, the other manifestations being referred to in antiphons at lauds and vespers, and the baptism celebrated on the following Sunday.

The Wise Men were known by a variety of names, standardized in the Middle Ages as Melchior, Caspar and Balthasar. Their gifts, which in the old dispensation had messianic significance, were also given symbolic values by the Fathers of the Church, gold being the tribute to Christ's kingship, frankincense to his divinity, and myrrh the forecast of his death. In England, following the example of the Three Kings, the sovereign presents gifts in the Chapel Royal of one of the palaces.

Epiphany came to be regarded as the climax and conclusion of the merrymaking associated with the traditional twelve days of Christmas.

Entries in the diary of Samuel Pepys (1633–1703) describe the revels which lasted until midnight, with music and dancing, and the division of the Twelfth Night cake so that the man who got the concealed bean and the woman the pea became respectively king and queen for the evening. Although in many places greenery and foliage were left until 2 February, the Purification of the Blessed Virgin Mary, it is now customary to take down decorations at Epiphany, marking the end of Christmastide.

Lent

ORIGINS   A season of prayer, penance and self-discipline, beginning on the Wednesday of the seventh week before Easter, precedes the joyful celebration of Christ's victory over death. Its origin is the pre-festival fast which at this time of the year was also observed by those to be initiated into full membership of the Christian community. This ceremony took place for preference at Easter because the rite was associated symbolically with Christ's death and resurrection. 'So by our baptism into his death we were buried with him, so that as Christ was raised from the dead by the Father's glorious power, we too should begin living a new life', Paul wrote to the Church in Rome (Rm 6:4). As the neophyte, the new convert, entered the water, he descended into the tomb, dead to the sinful world: he emerged born again into the world of light, 'illuminated' and 'enlightened'. He was given milk sweetened with honey to drink, foretaste of heaven, the allegorical Promised Land 'flowing with milk and honey', which historically the Israelites entered after their miraculous crossing of the River Jordan where, centuries later, Jesus was baptized.

In the second section of a treatise known as *The Teaching of the Twelve Apostles*, an early manual of discipline and practice, those about to be baptized (Greek *baptizein*: 'to dip') are bidden to fast for one or two days beforehand. To encourage them in their ordeal, the baptizer 'and any others who are able' are asked to fast with them. This short fast may have been the norm in many Churches but there were variations. At a crisis in the Quartodeciman controversy *c*.190, Irenaeus wrote to Victor, bishop of Rome, that 'some think that they ought to fast one day, others two, others even more'. He added: 'Some count their day as forty hours, day and night', seemingly a continuous fast in fulfilment of Jesus' prediction that there would be a time for mourning when the bridegroom of the parable was taken away, interpreted as the hours when Jesus was in the tomb (Mt 9:15). Tertullian compared this fast unfavourably with the longer one undertaken by Montanists, the apocalyptic ascetic sect which he had joined. St Hippolytus considered two days, or, for the sick, Saturday on bread and water, to be sufficient for Christians in Rome. Dionysius the Great (*d.*264), bishop of Alexandria, wrote that in his diocese there were some who did not fast at all; others who denied themselves on two, three or even four days before Easter; and some spiritual athletes who took only bread, salt and water at the ninth hour (3 p.m.) on the first four days of that week and then observed a total fast on Friday and Saturday.

By the fourth century an extended fast of forty days was usual. Canon 5 of the First Council of Nicaea (325) cannot be cited as evidence because there is uncertainty as to the meaning of the decision that one of the two annual provincial councils should be held 'before the fortieth', but forty days were commended by St Athanasius (*c.*296–373) in his *Festal Letters* and his near-contemporary, St Cyril (*c.*315–86), bishop of Jerusalem, told candidates that they had forty days of penitence to prepare themselves for baptism. This change from hours to days may have come about because it was noted that 'forty' in the Scriptures was associated with a time of sorrow or affliction before eventual joy. It was the period when flood waters covered the earth before Noah and his family reached dry land; Moses went without food and water for the same number of days as he wrote down the words of the Covenant; and Elijah walked through the desert for forty days until he reached the cave where he heard the 'still small voice' of God.

There was nevertheless a lack of uniformity throughout the Church because there were local differences as to which days in each week were to be designated fast days and the number of weeks over which they were to be distributed. Socrates (*c.*380–450), the Greek ecclesiastical historian, noted that in some places the season lasted six weeks, in others seven, yet it was everywhere called 'the forty-day fast'. 'It is indeed surprising,' he wrote, 'that thus differing in the number of days, they should give it a common name, but some assign one reason for it, others another, according to their several fancies.' Egeria, who was accustomed to forty days in her convent in the West, noted that the period extended over eight weeks in Jerusalem, presumably because eight Sundays and seven Saturdays being excluded from the count, there was fasting on five days of each of these weeks.

In general there were two methods of calculating the duration of the fast: the deduction of thirteen non-fasting days (seven Sundays and six Saturdays, but not Holy Saturday) from seven weeks, usual in the East; and the omission of six Sundays from a six-week season, as practised in Rome. Actually both methods yielded only thirty-six fasting days, which St

Gregory the Great, echoing John Cassian (*c*.360–435), the monk who drew up rules for the monastic life, called the Holy Tithe, one tenth of the year dedicated to God's service, after the example of the Israelites who had offered him one tenth of their produce. Following tradition, the Sunday after which this fast began was called *quadragesima*, translating Greek *tesserakostē*: 'fortieth', but the anomaly was apparent and eventually four days were added to make the number of fast days accord with the forty which Jesus spent in the wilderness: thus *quadragesima* came to mean not only the Sunday but also the season. From it were derived Romance names, e.g. Italian *quaresima*, Spanish *cuaresma*, French *carême*, Welsh *garawys* – whereas 'Lent' is derived from Old English *lencten*, 'spring', denoting the time of year.

When Wednesday before Quadragesima Sunday became *caput ieiunii*: 'the beginning of the fast', is uncertain but it is referred to in the mid-eighth-century Vatican manuscript of the Gelasian Sacramentary and was known to Amalarius of Metz in the ninth century. This arrangement was made obligatory by the Council of Meaux (846) and accepted wherever the Roman rite was adopted, although as late as the eleventh century the saintly Queen Margaret of Scotland (1045–93), a Saxon princess who had been nurtured in the Roman tradition, met considerable opposition when she tried to persuade her husband's subjects to observe the forty-day Lent which she had known in her homeland.

SEPTUAGESIMA   Until 1969, when the names were removed from the *Roman Missal*, the three Sundays before Lent were designated literally (although arithmetically correct only in the case of the third) Septuagesima, Sexagesima and Quinquagesima, 'seventieth', 'sixtieth' and 'fiftieth' days before Easter, a harmonious succession formed by analogy with Quinquagesima and constituting an independent pre-Lent season. As these Sundays were so named in the medieval Use of Sarum, the modification of the Roman rite used in the cathedral church of Salisbury which influenced the composition of the *First Prayer Book of Edward VI* (1549), the titles were retained and ultimately included in the nomenclature of the *Book of Common Prayer*. Reminiscent of their original autonomy are the subtitles in the *Alternative Service Book* Third, Second and Next before Lent for the Ninth to Seventh before Easter, when a new cycle of lections begins.

St Maximus (*d*.408 or 423), bishop of Turin, commended the three weeks encompassed by these Sundays as a pious but not obligatory time of abstinence. A more formal character was given to them by St Gregory the

Great when he composed intercessions to be said each day for the deliverance of Rome from marauding bands of Lombard soldiery. Thereafter a pre-Lent season with special prayers and readings became customary in monasteries under Roman obedience. The seventy days which began on Septuagesima Sunday were equated with the seventy sorrowful years which the Israelites spent in captivity by the waters of Babylon. 'How can we sing the Lord's song in a strange land?' lamented the Psalmist (Ps 137/136:4). The Lord's song, in the Christian liturgy, is Alleluia, 'Praise ye the Lord', sung before the gospel. Conforming to earlier monastic practice, Alexander III (1159–81) ordered that this joyful exclamation should be sung twice at the last office before Septuagesima Sunday and then replaced until Easter by a tract, a penitential chant. This is now the custom during Lent.

SHROVETIDE   The Lenten season begins after evening prayer on Shrove Tuesday, the last of the days of Shrovetide, traditionally the time set aside for confessing sins and being granted absolution before the long period of spiritual preparation and abstinence from certain foods. Used adjectivally in this context, 'shrove' is an alternative past participle for 'shriven', from the verb 'to shrive', meaning 'to write'. (Compare modern German *schreiben* and Dutch *schrijven*.) In medieval England a priest would hear a confession and, in theory if not in practice, write down, or prescribe, an appropriate penance. After absolution, the person was said to have been 'shriven'.

Shrove Tuesday was the last day for preparing dishes containing eggs, milk and cooking fat or butter, foods forbidden during Lent. These ingredients were therefore used up in pancakes or similar recipes. In France the day is called *mardi gras*, 'Fat Tuesday'. (It is said that the Butter Tower of Rouen Cathedral was built from money saved by not using butter in Lent.) Shrove Tuesday was also the last opportunity for eating meat (Latin *carnis*: 'flesh'), hence 'carnival' and related words in Romance languages (French *carnaval*, Italian *carnevale* or *carnelasciare*, medieval Spanish *carnestolendas*, Catalan *carnestoltes*), conveying the idea of 'taking away' or 'ceasing to eat' meat, became synonymous with revelry associated with the last opportunity for self-indulgence before the rigours of Lent.

ASH WEDNESDAY   A universal day of penitence which, depending on the date of Easter, may fall between 4 February and 11 March, Ash Wednesday derives its name from the rite of ashing, that is sprinkling on the head, or imposing on the forehead in the form of a cross, blessed ashes made from burnt branches of palm, olive or evergreens, according to region, carried the previous year in Palm Sunday processions. To each penitent, recalling God's admonition to Adam when he expelled him and Eve from the Garden of Eden, the celebrant says 'Remember, man, dust thou art and to dust thou shalt return'. An alternative formula, positive and expressive of the Lenten theme of reconciliation of man to God, echoing Jesus' first proclamation in Galilee, 'Repent, and believe in the gospel' (Mk I:15), is 'Turn away from sin and be faithful to the gospel'.

Ashes and sackcloth were biblical symbols of repentance. 'I abhor myself, and repent in dust and ashes', cried Job, sorrowful because he had questioned the inscrutable ways of God; and the king of Nineveh took off his robe, put on sackcloth and sat down in ashes when he called upon his people to renounce their evil ways. An early Jewish purification rite which used ashes of a red heifer without fault or blemish was seen to be perfected in Christ who, blameless as he was, offered himself to purge the consciences of sinners so that they could serve the living God (Hb 9:13–14). In this sense, ashes, as well as denoting repentance, also symbolize salvation through Christ's sacrifice of himself on the cross.

A requirement of the early medieval penitentiary code was that grave sinners who had been excluded from the sacraments but were deemed ready to seek forgiveness should come barefoot to church on the first day of Lent. After they had expressed their sorrow they had ashes sprinkled on their heads, or were handed a sackcloth garment covered in ashes, and were sent away to perform their allotted penances. Their relatives, who felt themselves contaminated by their kinsfolk's fall from grace, usually accompanied them and many voluntarily submitted to some form of discipline, wearing sackcloth in private or, as in parts of Germany, accepting the garment at a public ceremony. When frequent private confessions and shriving became more common, the individual use of sackcloth declined: instead the whole congregation was ashed. This rite was known to Aelfric (*c.*955–*c.*1020), the great English Benedictine scholar, and adopted in Rome about the same time. The Council of Benevento (1091) decreed that everyone, laity and clergy, should receive ashes on the first day of Lent.

The ceremony was abolished in England in January 1548 by order of the Regency Council of Edward VI and the name omitted at this point from the *Prayer Book of 1552*, to be restored as a subtitle to the First Day of Lent, 'commonly called Ash Wednesday', in the *Book of Common Prayer*. An order for the beginning of Lent with an introduction in which the president explains the meaning of the season was commended in 1986 by the House of Bishops of the General Synod of the Church of England.

46

A COMMINATION   A year after the Regency Council of Edward VI ordered the abolition of the ceremony for the blessing and imposition of ashes, the *Prayer Book of 1549* directed that on 'The First Daie of Lent commonly called Ashe-Wednesdaye' a bell should be rung after matins to summon the people to church. After the litany had been said in the midst of the church 'in English' (an important statement because Archbishop Cranmer had recently produced a translation), the priest was to read from the pulpit 'the general sentences of God's cursing against impenitent sinners', seven of which were derived from stern Deuteronomic texts (Dt 27:15–25). There followed a homily based on God's day of vengeance on obstinate sinners, the unmerciful, fornicators, idolaters, slanderers and drunkards, concluding with an exhortation to repentance and trust in Christ's infinite mercy. Priests, clerks and parishioners then knelt to say the penitential psalms, including *Miserere mei Deus*: 'Have mercy upon me, O God' (Ps 51/50), before the final prayers.

This new service, derived in part from the medieval rite of greater excommunication, was intended as a temporary expedient until 'the ancient lenten discipline of notorious sinners' was restored: 'which thing is much to be wished', it was stated in the Preface. This did not happen but the essentials of the service, no longer restricted to Ash Wednesday, were retained in the *Prayer Book of 1552*, where it was entitled 'A Commination against sinners' (Latin *comminari*, 'to warn', 'admonish'). Matthew Wren (1585–1667), bishop of Ely, whose suggestions influenced the revision of the *Book of Common Prayer*, supplied the explanatory clause, 'or a Denouncing of God's Anger and Judgements against Sinners', to be used not only on Ash Wednesday but also 'at all other times as the ordinary [i.e. the bishop] shall appoint'.

In 1928, when sentences like 'Cursed be he that removeth his neighbour's landmark' were thought to be no longer relevant to a modern industrialized society, proposals were made to replace uncompromisingly negative censures by the Beatitudes (Lk 6:20–26), but the entire service was omitted from the ill-fated Prayer Book rejected by Parliament and was not included in the *Alternative Service Book*. It is perhaps a matter for regret that the fine cadences of the original now rarely resound in parish churches.

LENTEN DISCIPLINE   During Lent the obligation of fasting, going without meals during the day, a continuation of the Jewish custom of taking a meal at sunset when fasting, and abstinence, avoiding certain foods, was strict and often heroic in observance, although, as Socrates noted, there was disagreement as to what could be consumed. 'Some', he wrote in his *Ecclesiastical History*, 'abstain from things that have life: others feed on fish only of all living creatures.' He was of the opinion that, as no written authority could be produced, the apostles had left each one to his own free will in the matter. Generally wine, flesh-meat, fish, eggs and 'foods made from milk' (Latin *laticinia*), cheese and butter, were forbidden. This regime was too severe for those under rule who were required to be present at long choir offices as well as performing fatiguing manual tasks. From the ninth century onwards dispensations for reasons of health became frequent for all: fish was allowed and flesh-meat on Sundays permitted. In the late Middle Ages, to avoid breaking the monastic rule that the fast should not be broken until after the Mass which followed None (the ninth hour reckoned from sunrise, i.e. about 3 p.m.), this office was moved to midday, which is the reason why this hour is now called 'noon'. To prevent exhaustion monks were permitted a collation, a light evening meal, so called because it was accompanied by readings from John Cassian's *Conferences* (Latin *collationes*), his conversations with Egyptian desert hermits.

Ash Wednesday, Good Friday and the other weekdays in Lent are traditional days of discipline and self-denial and were a legal requirement in England until 1863, although 'more honour'd in the breach than the observance'. Vestigial traces remain as folk customs among those whose religious allegiance is nominal, or non-existent, yet 'give up something for Lent' and eat hot cross buns and fish on Good Friday. The Roman Catholic law of fasting was redefined in the Apostolic Constitution *Paenitemini* of Paul VI in 1966. Those who have completed their twenty-first year, and up until the beginning of their sixtieth year, are allowed only one full meal a day but may take some refreshment morning and evening, the food consumed being in accordance with norms established locally by episcopal conferences.

It is often difficult in a secular society for Christians openly to practise such self-denial without appearing precious or kill-joys, refusing business luncheons or other forms of entertainment. Instead many choose to increase charitable giving, or to devote more time to serious reading and study groups. Whatever form their personal discipline may take, they are enjoined not to make it obvious or parade it as a virtue. 'Rend your hearts and not your garments,' cried Joel, the prophet. Jesus taught, 'When you fast, put scent on your head and wash your face, so that no one will know you are fasting except your Father who sees all that is done in secret' (Mt 6:17–18). He related the parable of the Pharisee who thanked God that he was not as

other men because he fasted twice a week and gave away a tenth of his
income, yet was inferior to the hated but humble tax-gatherer who could do
no more than beat his breast and exclaim, 'God be merciful to me, a sinner'
(Lk 18:9 14).

TEMPTATION IN THE WILDERNESS   The gospel reading
which epitomizes the meaning and spirit of Lent is the account of Jesus'
temptation, or testing-time (Latin *temptare*, 'to test'), when, immediately
after his baptism, he spent forty days fasting in the wilderness, an
uninhabited region east of Jordan, his spiritual trial there being linked
allegorically with the forty years during which the Israelites wandered in the
Sinai waste-land. It was said in the *Gospel of Mark* that in that desert, the
haunt of evil spirits, 'he was tempted by Satan'. The Gospels of *Matthew*
and *Luke* expand this statement, specifying three temptations, although not
in the same order (Mk I:12; Mt 4:1–11; Lk 4:1–13).

   If Jesus really were the Son of God, Satan argued, he could reveal his
supernatural powers in a series of dramatic actions. He could feed the
hungry by turning the stones of the desert into loaves of bread (a pun on
similar-sounding Hebrew words which is lost in translation); he could jump
unharmed from the pinnacle of the Temple, where it was believed the
Anointed One would appear; and, greatest temptation of all, he could
present himself as the warrior Messiah who would drive out the hated
Roman oppressors. From a high mountain, traditionally Jebel Quruntul
where the stone on which Jesus sat during this encounter may be seen by
visitors to the monastery, Satan showed him in a moment of time 'all the
kingdoms of the world' which he could subdue and rule, citing scripture for
his purpose. Jesus rebutted each quotation with texts from *Deuteronomy*.
His role was to be the servant of God, foretold by Isaiah, who would suffer
death but ultimately triumph. Medieval exegetes found in this episode both
warning and encouragement for those traversing the spiritual waste-land of
Lent, likened to the purgative way of the mystics, an interpretation which is
not without value today. Desert wild beasts represented besetting sins; three
trials to be overcome, proud ways to be defeated; angels who ministered to
Jesus, recalling the benign messengers who fed the Israelites, guarantors of
divine assistance to overcome temptation. That the devil departed from
Jesus 'for a season', until a more opportune moment, was seen as a warning
always to be on guard against his future assaults.

LENTEN VEILING   In many churches during Lent there is visible evidence of the austerity of the season. Purple, or in some places violet or blue, is the prevailing liturgical colour; there is a notable absence of flowers; and, although this is no longer obligatory, crucifixes, statues and pictures may be covered with purple veiling. In Roman Catholic churches, should the local conference of bishops decide, veiling is required from the eve of Passion Sunday, the Sunday next before Easter, until the last Old Testament reading, psalm and prayer of the Easter Vigil. To enhance the mood of reflective silence, the organ or other instrument is not played, or is used only to accompany singing or chanting by the choir or celebrant. The *Gloria in excelsis deo* is omitted and Alleluia replaced by an acclamation, or verse before the reading of the Gospel. There is a Proper, a variable part appropriate to the season, for Mass or Eucharist and frequent attendance is encouraged. The rubric, the ritual direction for the First Day of Lent in the *Book of Common Prayer*, 'this collect to be read every day of Lent', indicates that English bishops at the Conference in March 1661, which met at the Savoy in the Strand, London, also intended a daily service to be held.

A Lenten veil (Latin *velum quadragesimale*: 'Lenten covering') made of unbleached linen was drawn across the sanctuary, the east end of the church containing the altar, in the Middle Ages, 'because', wrote William Durandus (*c.*1230–96), bishop of Mende, 'Jesus hid himself and left the Temple' (Jn 8:59). This was done in some churches after the first Sunday in Lent, in others after the fifth, then called Passion Sunday, because, it was said, by delivering himself up to be scourged, Jesus temporarily divested himself of his divinity. The veil was withdrawn temporarily after the Saturday vigil, or after the reading of the gospel at Mass, so that the congregation should understand how the darkness of the Old Law was overcome by the light of the New. It was also pulled aside on the festival of one of the greater saints, the so-called 'feast of nine lessons', and in Holy Week as the words, 'and the veil of the Temple was rent in the midst', were declaimed (Lk 23–45). Durandus also noted that a curtain sometimes concealed the quire where the clergy sat in their stalls from the laity in the nave, the body of the church, because it symbolized the gates of Paradise shut against Adam and Eve after their expulsion for disobedience. At Mass it was withdrawn as a reminder that Christ opened the door of the Kingdom of Heaven, represented by the sanctuary.

LENTEN ARRAY   Medieval churches were decorated with pictures, ornaments and carvings, 'the lessons and scriptures of the laity', said Durandus. Behind the altar the reredos, painted wooden panels, carvings or sculptures, depicted saints and scriptural episodes. On the rood-screen, the partition between nave and chancel, the part reserved for the clergy, was the rood (Old English *rod*: 'cross'), a crucifix flanked by St Mary the Virgin and St John. These, and processional crosses, were shrouded in unbleached linen, according to Durandus to move the faithful to greater penance because they were deprived 'of the consolation which the sight of these holy images always brings to the soul'.

This custom, known as Lenten array, ceased in England when 'images', meaning all visual representations in church, were condemned in the Thirty-Nine Articles, the Anglican doctrinal statement of 1563, as incitement to idolatry, and during outbursts of iconoclasm were covered in whitewash, defaced or removed. Influenced by the medievalism of the Oxford Movement and the Cambridge Camden Society, Lenten array was revived in the later nineteenth century in many churches, particularly those built during the Gothic Revival when decoration was again in vogue. The veil often bore an emblem indicating the object which it concealed.

MOTHERING SUNDAY   Festal joy returns briefly on the fourth Sunday when rose-pink vestments may replace violet or purple. This is *Laetare* Sunday, named after the first Latin word of the introit, or entrance antiphon, 'Rejoice, Jerusalem, be glad for her, all you who love her!' (Is 66:10). Until 1969, when Roman Catholic reforms reinstated all Sundays as festivals, it was also known as Refreshment Sunday because relaxation of Lenten abstinence was permitted, a boon confirmed by the gospel then read, retained in the *Book of Common Prayer*, which related the miraculous feeding of the five thousand (Jn 6:1–14). The multitude had forsaken the comforts of their homes, in the same way as the faithful had abandoned worldly pleasures, and Jesus refreshed them with bread and fish, which are eucharistic symbols.

Another name is Mid-Lent Sunday (French *mi-carême*), seemingly inappropriate because the half-way mark is actually the previous Thursday. It may reflect an earlier method of computing the duration of Lent or, more likely, a transference to Sunday, because breaking fast on a weekday would relax Lenten discipline, an arrangement justified by the gospel then read beginning 'When the festival was half over, Jesus went to the Temple and began to teach' (Jn 7:14). This was the Feast of Tabernacles, the Jewish harvest festival which lasted eight days and was therefore half over by the fourth, understood as signifying allegorically Mid-Lent Sunday.

Popularly, in England, this is Mothering Sunday, although it is uncertain how it acquired that title. A possible explanation is that the pope said Mass on that day at the basilica of Santa Croce in Gerusalemme ('Holy-Cross-in-Jerusalem') which contained relics of the Holy Cross acquired in Jerusalem by Empress Helena, mother of Constantine the Great. The epistle quoted St Paul's reference to the Heavenly Jerusalem, 'mother of us all' (Ga 4:26). In the same way, the local cathedral, mother-church of the diocese, was the focus of worship on this Sunday. An appendix to the decisions of the Third Lateran Council (1167) designated 'mother-churches' those where, as distinct from private chapels, baptisms took place, and were attended by the faithful on this day as a reminder of their baptism.

Whatever the reason, this Sunday was associated in people's minds with the idea of 'mother'. It became customary in England for servants and apprentices to be given time off to attend with their families the church where they had been baptized. They presented their mothers with a cake made of eggs, butter and simnel, finest flour, ingredients which were not otherwise used during Lent.

THE GOLDEN ROSE   An ancient ceremony which originally took place in the church of Santa Croce in Gerusalemme on the fourth Sunday in Lent, but is now performed in the Vatican, is the blessing of the Golden Rose, a bejewelled ornament in the form of a thorny stem with leaves and flowers, the rose at the top concealing a container perfumed with musk. Pope St Leo IX (1049–54) spoke of the rite as age-old but originally it may have been connected with the arrival of spring when flowering branches were carried by the pope from the Lateran Palace, his official residence, to Santa Croce in Gerusalemme where he celebrated Mass. Medieval devotion to St Mary the Virgin, 'Rose of Sharon', may have caused the substitution of her emblem, also the symbol of spiritual joy. The early association with Santa Croce is recalled in the prayer that the faithful 'may show forth with a sincere heart the joys of that Jerusalem which is above and is our mother'.

Until 1307, when the pope left Rome to begin the 'Babylonian Captivity' in Avignon which lasted until 1377, the rose was presented to the prince who held the pope's stirrup and helped him to dismount. Later it was sent as a gift to a sovereign, city or institution worthy of honour. Henry VIII, England's 'Defender of the Faith', received three roses from successive popes, and Julius III sent a rose to Mary Tudor in 1555. Queens have been recipients because of the flower's Marian symbolism, among them Mary Cassimir, Queen of Poland, honoured with her husband John Sobieski by Innocent XI in 1684 for raising the siege of Vienna, invested by the Turks. A city or an institution may also receive the gift, which is retained as a token of special honour. If the rose is not awarded it remains in the Vatican and is blessed each year until a suitable occasion presents itself.

TENEBRAE   Although modified since 1955, the ancient office for matins and lauds of the last three days of Holy Week (at one time to encourage lay attendance anticipated on the three preceding evenings) deserves mention because of the intrinsic value of the ceremonial and the profound beauty of the music which survives in the works of notable composers like Orlando de Lassus (1532–94). Memorable too is the setting by Tomás Luis de Victoria (1548–1611) of the Lamentations, verses from the book of that name attributed to the prophet Jeremiah (7th century BC) which were interpreted as referring to Christ's Passion.

Tenebrae (from the Latin for 'darkness'), the popular name for the office, is usually explained by the fact that the service ended in the dark, but it is more likely to be derived from the text 'and there was a darkness over all the earth' at the sixth hour on Good Friday (Lk 23:44) or from 'the darkness could not overwhelm the Light of the World' (Jn 1:5). Fifteen candles were placed on a triangular candlestick and fourteen were extinguished one by one after each psalm was chanted. The last candle was left alight and hidden, usually behind the altar during the singing of the Benedictus, Zechariah's song of thanksgiving at the birth of John the Baptist (Lk 1:68–79), to symbolize the entombment of Christ. When the signal for departure was given, the candle was brought out and placed on the candlestick to provide light as the congregation dispersed but interpreted as anticipating the resurrection.

The ceremonial is now inappropriate as the office takes place during the day, but some of the material remains in the Liturgy of the Hours (1971).

THE SCRUTINIES   In the early days of the Church the model for the initiation of adults was the baptism in water by the roadside of the chief treasurer of the Queen of Ethiopia to whom Philip the Deacon had explained the Good News of Jesus, the prophesied Messiah (Ac 8:36–9). A river, a stretch of running water, or even a bath-house sufficed for the rite but, as St Justin Martyr explained, before the neophytes were led 'to a place where there is water', they had received instruction in the faith and had pledged themselves to live according to Christian precepts. From the *Treatise on the Apostolic Tradition*, ascribed to St Hippolytus, it may be deduced that prospective converts were also carefully examined beforehand as to their motives and their way of life, particularly if they were sculptors, painters, charioteers, gladiators or astrologers, occupations forbidden to Christians. By the fourth century the period of instruction had been formalized. Catechumens ('hearers of the word of God') were required to give their names at least forty days in advance, usually at the beginning of the Lenten period, as Easter was preferred for the ceremony. When enrolled, after they had satisfied the bishop of their sincerity, they received instruction during a course of formal lectures and were ceremonially examined as to their knowledge of the Creed and the Lord's Prayer.

The Catholic faith finally triumphed over the ancient religions during the reign of Theodosius the Great (379–95), thus completing the process which the Emperor Constantine had begun early that century. Political and personal advancement was thereafter bound up with becoming a Christian. It was therefore essential that converts should demonstrate their sincere conversion in a public ceremony. In 385 Pope St Siricius (384–99) ordered that those to be baptized at Easter or Pentecost should appear with their sponsors on certain solemn occasions, called 'scrutinies' (Latin *scrutinia*: 'investigations'), so that the bishop could be sure that they had renounced evil practices associated with paganism and the mystery religions and were conversant with the teachings of the Church. These public examinations, formalized by the Synod of Rome *c*.402, were held three times during the forty days leading up to Easter or Pentecost in the basilica of St John Lateran.

The need for these Scrutinies diminished in succeeding centuries as infant baptism, usually performed eight days after birth, and thus not tied to a particular season, became the norm. In the twentieth century, in a secularized society, this was no longer the case, many adult converts coming from non-Christian backgrounds or, in the mission field, from animistic and other religions. For these reasons the Roman Catholic Church in 1962 restored the Catechumenate, formal public preparation for baptism, and in 1972 issued the *Order of Christian Initiation of Adults* which, although reviving many of the features of the ancient Scrutinies, no longer regards them as examinations but as stages towards integration within a Christian community.

Applicants are welcomed, allotted sponsors, signed with a cross to show that they are under the protection of Christ, and after a period of instruction, present themselves on the First Sunday of Lent as *electi*: 'chosen ones', signifying that they have been chosen by Christ 'to be holy and spotless, and to live through love in his presence' (Eph I:4). After further instruction and study they again appear on the Third, Fourth and Fifth Sundays for ceremonies which recall the ancient *traditio symboli*: 'giving of the Creed', when they were taught the Lord's Prayer and the articles of the faith, so that they could 'hand them back' (*redditio*), that is, repeat them in public, before baptism. In theory, as in the ancient Church, catechumens should be dismissed before the beginning of the Eucharist, attendance at that part of the service being reserved to the baptized, but this is now mostly considered pastorally unacceptable.

Gospel readings for these Scrutiny Sundays are on the theme of salvation through baptism, for the Lord God said, 'I shall pour clean water over you and you will be cleansed . . . I shall give you a new heart and put a new spirit in you' (Ez 36:25–6). Jesus told the Samaritan woman who came to draw water at Jacob's Well, 'anyone who drinks the water that I shall give will never be thirsty again: the water that I shall give will turn into a spring inside him, welling up to eternal life' (Jn 4:14). The beggar who was blind from birth told his astonished neighbours, 'A man called Jesus said to me, "Go to the pool of Siloam and wash"; so I went, and when I washed I could see' (Jn 9:11).

Holy Week

For St John Chrysostom the last seven days of Christ's redeeming work on earth constituted the Great Week because 'great things were wrought at that time by the Lord'. Egeria, who in her convent in the West knew it as Paschal Week, noted that in Jerusalem it was called the Greater Week, a title which is also found in Roman ecclesiastical usage. In England it was for centuries Passion Week but this was later superseded by the now familiar Holy Week, as in many other languages, expressive of the sanctity of the time.

From the mid-fourth century onwards, the Quartodecimans defeated, and Easter Sunday universally recognized as the festival of Christ's resurrection, Holy Week, comprising the last days of Lent, which now ends at evening prayer on Holy Thursday, was endowed with distinctive liturgical features. Candidates received their final preparation for baptism; fasting and private devotions were intensified; and each step in Jesus' progress to Calvary was recalled and, where appropriate, re-enacted. In Jerusalem it was possible to do this at sites traditionally identified and shown to pilgrims from the second century onwards and where the Emperor Constantine, determined that the new religion which he favoured should be worthily represented, had caused fine buildings to be constructed.

Elsewhere appropriate lections at monastic and church services emphasized the historical and commemorative aspects of each day.

This continues to be the case in the Catholic tradition in which there is a proper Mass for the first three weekdays, the most ancient being that for Wednesday, popularly known as Spy Wednesday because it was then that Judas agreed to betray his master for thirty pieces of silver. In the Anglican Communion, suitable epistles and gospel readings from one of the passion narratives allow for a daily eucharistic service where this is desired.

The reform of the Holy Week liturgy initiated in 1951 by Pius XII and similar revisions undertaken in many other Churches, eliminated non-essentials and re-emphasized the prime position of Holy Week in the ecclesiastical and devotional calendar. As St Leo the Great prayed, 'Let trespasses be forgiven; offences forgotten; revenge stifled; that this sacred festival may, by divine and human favours, find us all happy and innocent.'

PASSION SUNDAY: PALM SUNDAY   The sixth Sunday in Lent, the beginning of Holy Week, is entitled Passion Sunday because it is devoted to the contemplation of the 'suffering' (Latin *passio*) of Jesus from the time of his agonized prayers on the Mount of Olives until his final hours on the cross. The intention, beautifully expressed in the *Book of Common Prayer*, for the Sunday next before Easter is 'that we may both follow the example of his patience [Latin *patientia*: 'calm endurance'] and also be made partakers of his resurrection'. Red, symbolizing martyrdom and victory over death, is the liturgical colour of the day.

Before the main eucharistic service, the congregation assembles at a convenient place away from or near the entrance to the church for the 'Commemoration of the Lord's Entry into Jerusalem' when, according to the Gospel of John, 'the people took branches of palm trees and went out to meet him' (Jn 12:13). From this event is derived the traditional name for the day, Palm Sunday, suppressed in England by Order in Council in January 1549 because reformers objected to clergy and people, bearing palms or other greenery, escorting the eucharistic Host (the consecrated Bread) displayed in a monstrance, probably the most popular of medieval outdoor festivals. It is suggested that in England the churchyard cross originally marked the starting-point of the procession which moved around the perimeter to the church door where it was received by the choir singing Zechariah's prophecy, 'Behold, thy king cometh, humble and riding on an ass' (Zc 9:9).

At present the congregation may carry palms, hazel twigs or pussy willow, according to region and seasonal availability, but usually they hold up to be blessed strips of palm leaf formed into the shape of a cross which they then keep at home until the next Ash Wednesday as a sign of Christ's presence. As they move into the church they sing the triumphal psalms, 'Gates, lift high your heads . . . and the king of glory shall enter' (Ps 24/23:7); and 'Clap your hands all peoples, acclaim God with shouts of joy' (Ps 47/46:1). Also sung is 'All glory, laud [i.e. praise] and honour', the hymn composed by St Theodulf of Orléans (c.750–821).

In this hymn, the acclamation of the Redeemer, 'to whom innocent children sang fervent Hosanna', felicitously rendered by J.M. Neale (1816–66) as, 'to whom the lips of children made sweet hosannas ring', poses a problem because children are not mentioned at this point in the canonical narratives. This is nevertheless an ancient tradition, echoed in the antiphon, 'The children of the Hebrews' and depicted on icons and in early Western art where children are to be seen throwing down branches from trees which line the roadside. A pilgrim from Bordeaux in 333 was shown, according to his account, 'the palm tree from which children took branches and strewed them in Christ's path'.

This could be the transposition of the next episode when, in the Temple, to the discomfort of the priests, children shouted 'Hosanna to the son of David' and Jesus quoted a version of the psalm, 'Out of the mouths of babes and sucklings thou hast perfected praise' (Ps 8:2). Curiously, however, Egeria, describing the Palm Sunday procession in Jerusalem, said that before it moved off down the Mount of Olives to the city gates, 'the passage from the gospel is read, where children carrying branches and palms met the Lord'. This may be a reference, not to a canonical Gospel, but to an early polemical work known as the *Acts of Pilate* in which a messenger reports that he saw Jesus 'sitting on an ass and the children of the Hebrews held branches in their hands and cried out; and others spread their garments before him'. Evidently, even at this early period, the idiom meaning 'Hebrew people' was understood literally as 'children'.

In the revised rite non-essential customs, such as halting the procession at the church door, representing the city gates, while a sub-deacon knocked with the foot of the processional cross to demand entry for the King of Glory, have been eliminated. Discouraged also is the somewhat hilarious practice in some English rural parishes of leading a donkey into church. Emphasis is not now on the mimetic representation of a past event but on its spiritual meaning, the joyful reception of the one who will lead the faithful into the heavenly city, the New Jerusalem.

The theme of the Mass which follows the procession is the ultimate victory of the servant of God who, as prophesied by Isaiah, would suffer torture and death: 'I have offered my back to those who struck me, my cheeks to those who plucked my beard; I have not turned my face away from insult and spitting. The Lord God comes to my help . . . I have set my face like flint and know that I shall not be put to shame' (Is 50:5–7). As Paul wrote to the Christians at Philippi, Jesus took the form of a slave and accepted a slave's death, 'death on a cross . . . and for this God raised him on high . . .' (Ph 2:7–9).

The gospel for this Sunday takes the form of the dramatic declamation of 'The Passion of our Lord Jesus Christ' from one of the Evangelists. (In the *Book of Common Prayer*, as formerly in the Roman rite, the appropriate passage from the *Gospel of Matthew* is appointed to be read.) This is the continuation of the medieval custom of the plainchant singing of a Passion narrative, at first by a deacon who altered the pitch of his voice to distinguish between narrative and direct speech, and later responsorially, a deacon acting as narrator and the choir assuming other roles. Greater variety was achieved with the introduction of polyphony, three clerics being involved as well as the choir. Sixtus V (1585–90), a reforming pope and patron of the arts, ordered his court musician to produce the definitive version of the tones to be used.

Present practice is for the celebrant or a priest to take the part of Jesus; clerics or lay persons the roles of the Evangelist, or of individual characters, and the choir or congregation the crowd. It is customary to kneel for a moment at the words, 'yielded up his spirit', or 'breathed his last', according to the version appointed for the day.

In the Lutheran church, the narrative was interspersed with devotional arias and meditations by the choir. Notable composers of settings for these Passions are Heinrich Schütz (1586–1672), Johann Sebastian Bach (1685–1750) and Georg Philipp Telemann (1681–1767).

MAUNDY THURSDAY   In the Middle Ages the Thursday of Holy Week was known as Paschal Thursday or 'the Thursday before Easter', a title retained in the *Book of Common Prayer*. Later it was called Holy Thursday, but in England Maundy Thursday, a title derived, by way of Old French *mandé*, from the Latin *mandatum*: 'command', the first word of the antiphon, *mandatum novum do vobis*: 'A new commandment I give unto you', based on the words in Jesus' farewell discourse (Jn 13:14) which followed his acted parable when, girding a towel about him like a servant, he washed and wiped his disciples' feet.

This courtesy was usually offered to a guest by female slaves, or if there were none, by women of the family. (Paul approved of widows 'who have washed the saints' feet' (I Tm 5:10), presumably before an *agape*: 'love feast'.) It has also been suggested that Jesus was not assuming a slave's role but inverting the custom (for which there is no first-century evidence) of a rabbi's followers washing his feet. In either case, by making this dramatic gesture during, not before, supper, Jesus was impressing on his disciples his law of love, that by humbling themselves they should show their love for each other as he had loved them, 'even unto death'.

As an act of humility, Benedictine abbots followed Jesus' example and washed the feet of their guests. The ceremony was introduced at an early period into the Gallic liturgy and was evidently known in Spain when, because it had been neglected, the seventeenth Synod of Toledo (694) ordered priests, under penalty of two months excommunication, to see that it was regularly performed. It was introduced into the Roman rite in the twelfth century when monastic influence prevailed in the Holy See. When the pope washed the feet of thirteen poor priests, the addition to the symbolic twelve disciples at the Last Supper was explained either as representing St Matthias, who replaced Judas, or Paul, 'called to be an apostle'. Another version was that the thirteenth recalled the angel (or Christ himself) who appeared when St Gregory the Great (590–604) was at table on Holy Thursday.

Monarchs, notably Queen Margaret of Scotland (1046–93) and St Louis of France (1214–70), were accustomed to wash the feet of selected paupers. In England an almoner (literally one who dispenses alms) scented with rose-water the feet of those chosen to appear before Queen Elizabeth I. The last English king to perform this humble duty was the unfortunate James I (1685–88). Since the Glorious Revolution, British rulers, or their representatives, attend a Maundy service in an appointed church or cathedral. The distribution of Maundy Money, newly-minted coins, one for each year of the sovereign's age, replaces foot-washing.

A rite for which there is now no provision was the service for the reconciliation of public penitents, who since Ash Wednesday, or even earlier, had been deprived of the sacraments. On Holy Thursday, barefoot, dressed in penitential garb, the men with hair and beard uncut, and having undergone a course of instruction and performed their allotted penances, they prostrated themselves at the church porch during the singing of the

Litany. There they were visited three times by deacons bearing messages of hope before being led to the bishop, who advanced half-way down the nave to meet them. After a lengthy address on the forgiveness of sins, prayers, the singing of the *Miserere*, 'Lord, have mercy', and other psalms, the formula of reconciliation was pronounced and the male penitents retired to have their hair and beards cut (which may explain the old name 'Shere [i.e. 'cutting'] Thursday') and to dress themselves once more in ordinary garments or white robes before attending Mass. As private confession and absolution became more general, this public rite fell into disuse but survives in the papal blessing, originally given only on this day, to the crowds assembled in St Peter's Square, Rome.

The Blessing of the Chrism, a continuation of an ancient rite, the renewal of the supply of oils to be used to anoint those to be baptized at Easter, now takes place on the morning of Holy Thursday in the cathedral where the bishop blesses three oils. Two of these are composed of olive oil, one to be used in baptism, the other for the unction of the sick and infirm. The third, called the chrism (Greek *chrisma*: 'oil of anointing'), is an ointment based on olive oil to which balsam or some other perfume is added, symbolizing 'the sweet savour of Christ'. These oils are kept in a chrismatory, a casket of silver or brass. As the oils are carried to the altar to be consecrated, the ancient hymn, *O Redemptor*: 'O Redeemer of mankind, receive the hymn of those who sing thy praise' by Venantius Fortunatus (*c*.530–*c*.610), bishop of Poitiers, may be sung. The blessing of the oils, necessary although it may be, is now incidental to the main purpose of the morning gathering: to emphasize the nature and duties of the priesthood. The bishop invites his clergy, in the presence of the assembled congregation, to renew their commitment to their calling and to pray that he himself may faithfully fulfil the apostolic office entrusted to him.

Easter

THREE HOLY DAYS   The ecclesiastical year reaches its climax at the Easter *Triduum*: 'three days' when Christ's victory over sin and death is celebrated in the form of a three-act drama. It opens with Jesus, obedient to his Father's will, accepting his destiny; declines into bathos when, all seeming lost, he is crucified and buried; and concludes triumphantly with his mighty resurrection. 'For as in Adam all die. . . . even so in Christ shall all be made alive' (I Cor 15:22).

Liturgically this drama begins on Holy Thursday evening and ends with evening prayer on Easter Sunday. Thus the Easter festival is restored to its original form as a unitive celebration of the fact that the sacrifice on the cross is not the end but the prologue to the Resurrection, the central mystery of the Christian faith. In the words of St Leo the Great, Easter is 'the feast of feasts'.

MASS OF THE LORD'S SUPPER   St Paul, writing to Christians at Corinth (I Cor II: 23–6), gave the earliest account of the institution of the Eucharist, 'the breaking of the bread', the supreme rite of the faith. At supper on the night that he was betrayed, Jesus performed two symbolic acts: he took bread and broke it, saying that it was his body; and holding a cup of wine he pronounced it the blood of the new covenant, the new contract between God and man. After each action he said, 'Do this in remembrance of me'.

Principal mealtimes in the ancient world were around noon and in the evening, but on fast days, especially during Lent, many early Christians went without food until the ninth hour (around 3 p.m.). Thus on Holy Thursday they were obliged to prolong their fast until the evening when the Eucharist commemorating the Last Supper took place. The solution, approved by the Council of Carthage (397) and at first followed in other parts of the West, was, exceptionally, to make this the one day in the year when those who had earlier broken their fast were allowed to take communion. This mitigation was later disallowed but to avoid discomfiture the Mass was moved to a more convenient hour, earlier in the day. In 1955 it was restored to its rightful place in the evening.

As this is a joyful occasion, the cross is veiled in white; white vestments are worn; 'Glory to God in the highest' is sung; and church bells are rung in honour of the institution of the Eucharist. An ancient name for the festival, attested in homilies attributed to St Eligius (c.590–660), patron saint of metalworkers, was 'Birthday of the Chalice', possibly a reference to the verse in the responsorial psalm, 'I will raise the cup of salvation' (Ps 116/115:13).

After a homily or sermon, the celebrant may re-enact Jesus' lesson in humility and service by ceremonially washing and wiping the feet of persons selected from the congregation. As he does so the hymn *Ubi caritas*: 'Where there is love, God is there' is sung.

The mood changes after the prayer which follows the consecration of the Eucharist and the distribution of communion. With the greatest reverence the Blessed Sacrament is carried in procession to the place of repose, usually a decorated side-chapel, as the first four stanzas of the hymn, *Pange, lingua gloriosi corporis mysterium*: 'Of the glorious body telling', by St Thomas Aquinas (1225–74) are sung. As the ciborium is set in its place, the hymn is concluded with the singing of the last two verses, beginning 'therefore we, before him bending'.

The sacred ministers then withdraw to the sacristy and the altar in the church is stripped, often to the words of the chilling twenty-second psalm, 'My God, my God, look upon me; why hast thou forsaken me?'. The church is left bare of all ornament, dark and silent, empty except for those who remain until midnight in meditation before the Blessed Sacrament. For the next two days no bell sounds but some places may observe the ancient practice of announcing services and devotions by the *strepitacula*, a noise made by a clapper-board, a survival from the time before the introduction of bells in the late fifth century.

GOOD FRIDAY   Good Friday (Holy Friday in other languages), the traditional English name for the day devoted to the contemplation of Jesus' suffering and death on the cross, at first sight seems paradoxical. Nevertheless, as the collect in the *Book of Common Prayer* avers, it is 'good' for mankind because, 'through his death, he opened to us the gates of everlasting life'. This consoling thought is kept in mind throughout the sombre ceremonies of the day.

THREE HOURS DEVOTION   From noon until three o'clock, or at later hours should social conditions require it, many churches hold a service which originated as a devotional exercise instituted by Alonso Mexía, a Jesuit, in Peru after an earthquake had devastated Lima in 1687. Promoted in England by the Anglican priest A.H. Mackonochie (1825–87), who suffered persecution for his ritualism and his adherence to the Catholic tradition, it later appealed to many evangelical congregations and became their main Good Friday observance.

The service is usually structured around the seven words which Jesus uttered as he hung on the cross: 'Father forgive them' (Lk 23:34); 'Today shalt thou be with me in paradise' (Lk 23:43); 'Woman behold thy son!' (Jn 19:30); 'My God, my God, why hast thou forsaken me?' (Mt 27:46); 'I thirst' (Jn 19:28); 'It is finished' (Jn 19:30); 'Father into thy hands I commend my spirit' (Lk 23:46). (Notable musical settings of these words are by Heinrich Schütz (*c.*1645) and Charles François Gounod (1855).) Interspersed are short addresses, hymns and periods for meditation and prayers.

CELEBRATION OF THE LORD'S PASSION   'It is not fitting that we should celebrate a feast on the day on which the bridegroom is taken away from us', wrote Tertullian (*c.*160–*c.*225). In accordance with the tradition of the ancient Church, the sacraments are not celebrated on Good Friday nor on Holy Saturday, the eve of Easter, when Jesus' body rested in the tomb. The altar remains bare and unadorned, without cloths, candles or cross.

Towards three o'clock in the afternoon (later, if for pastoral convenience), the Lord's Passion is celebrated. It begins with the Liturgy of the Word, one of the readings being the fourth Suffering Servant song (Is 52:13–53:2) which lists the indignities inflicted on 'a man of sorrows, acquainted with grief'. The responsorial psalm has the haunting refrain, 'Father, into your hands I commend my spirit' (Ps 31/30:5). The gospel is the dramatic declamation of 'The Passion of our Lord Jesus Christ according to John' (Jn 18:1–19:42), the various parts being taken by priest, narrator, choir and congregation.

Wide-ranging intercessions for all sorts and conditions of men and their needs then follow: prayers for the unity of Christians; for those who do not believe in God, 'that they may find him by sincerely following all that is right'; and for those who believe in God but not in Christ. Mercifully, the prayer for the Jewish people, 'the first to hear the word of God', has been modified to express the wish that 'they may continue to grow in the love of his name and faithfulness to his covenant', a great improvement on the collect in the *Book of Common Prayer* which begs mercy for 'all Jews, Turks, Infidels and Hereticks'.

VENERATION OF THE CROSS   The second part of the service is centred on the veneration of the cross, once inelegantly called 'creeping to the cross' because, in the Middle Ages and later, the devout approached it on their knees. According to St Cyril (*c.*315–86), bishop of Jerusalem, this devotion came about as the result of the diffusion 'throughout the world' of relics of the cross which was discovered when the Emperor Constantine ordered excavations at Golgotha, the site of the crucifixion. Egeria related that, at the Good Friday service held there, deacons kept careful watch over the wood of the cross, enshrined in a silver-gilt box and placed before the bishop, because on one occasion a worshipper, instead of kissing the relic, had bitten off a fragment and made away with it, presumably to dispose of it at a profit.

An eighth-century *Comes*, a book containing lections to be read at

Mass, discovered in the library of the Benedictine abbey of Einsiedeln, Switzerland, indicates that the pope, carrying a relic of the cross, would lead barefoot a procession from St John Lateran to the nearby Santa Croce in Gerusalemme where the fragment was venerated. This basilica, now with an imposing baroque façade, stands on the site of the Sessorian palace, once the residence of St Helena, mother of the Emperor Constantine, who constructed there a private chapel, built on earth transported from the Mount of Olives, in order to house a thorn from the crown placed on Jesus' head, a nail, and three pieces of the wood of the cross. These relics are preserved in a modern chapel off the left aisle.

From Rome the veneration of the cross spread to other localities, whether or not churches there possessed relics, a plain cross or a crucifix being acceptable substitutes. In England it was one of the liturgical observances included in the *Regularis Concordia*, a monastic code attributed to St Ethelwold (*c*.912–84) and approved by the Synod of Winchester (*c*.970). Abolished at the time of the Reformation as one of the ceremonies which, according to the Thirty-Nine Articles, 'did more confound and darken, than declare and set forth Christ's benefits to us', it was revived in the nineteenth century in many Anglican churches influenced by the Oxford Movement for Catholic renewal.

A cross, escorted by two ministers or acolytes bearing lighted candles, is now carried in procession to the altar and is lifted up three times as the one who carries it proclaims, 'This is the wood of the cross', to which the response is, 'Come, let us worship'. If the cross is veiled, the upper part is first uncovered, then the right arm and then the whole cross. These symbolic actions represent the revelation of the Gospel, first to the disciples, then to the people of Jerusalem at Pentecost, and then to the whole world.

The cross is held, or laid down at the entrance to the sanctuary where it is venerated, either by genuflecting or kissing it, according to local custom. During the veneration the *Improperia*: 'Reproaches', are chanted antiphonally. These are based on incidents in which God has shown mercy to his people, but they, in return, have inflicted grievous injuries on Christ. Also sung is *Crux fidelis*: 'Faithful Cross', by Venantius Fortunatus (530–609).

The day ends with a subdued, prayerful Holy Communion. A cloth is spread on the altar; a book is placed on it; a ciborium containing the Blessed Sacrament is brought from the place where it was laid on Maundy Thursday night; the Lord's Prayer is said; communion distributed; and, after concluding prayers, all depart silently.

THE EASTER VIGIL   At nightfall on the seventh day, when according to Jewish reckoning the sabbath ends and the first day of the week begins, early Christians assembled for a nocturnal meeting which opened, as did the Judaic 'Praise of the Lord God', with the solemn lighting of the evening lamp, prelude to a vigil, a night-watch, in the expectation that Christ would return at midnight. In course of time vigils, as well as preceding the Sunday Eucharist, were also held before major festivals and many saints' days. Solemn vigils are now restricted in the Roman rite to Christmas, Easter and Pentecost.

The Easter vigil, which St Augustine of Hippo called 'mother of all holy vigils', after being put back successively to the afternoon, midday, and, in 1570, officially to the morning, was restored in 1951 to its rightful place, the night of Holy Saturday. It begins with the lighting and blessing of the 'new fire', a rite which may have originated in Ireland where it had legendary associations with St Patrick. It was adapted into the Roman liturgy in the twelfth century. Outside the church, around a charcoal brazier (unless a bonfire is possible), priest and people are assembled, a minister bearing a large Easter (or Paschal) candle made of unbleached wax, symbolizing Christ's virginal conception, because bees were thought to reproduce by parthenogenesis. The fire is kindled, anciently by striking a flint on stone, and blessed. The celebrant then cuts a cross on the candle and inscribes at the top *A* and at the bottom *ω*, alpha and omega, the first and last letters of the Greek alphabet, 'Christ yesterday and today, the beginning and the end'. The four numerals of the current year are then traced between the arms.

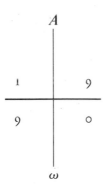

Five grains of incense, representing the five wounds of Christ, may be inserted in the wax, a practice which appears to have arisen from the misconstruction of the Latin words *hoc incensum*: 'this lighted candle', as 'this incense'.

Like the pillar of fire which went before the Israelites (Ex 13:22), the candle is borne into the darkened church where the congregation light their candles from it. Three times it is lifted up to the chant, 'Christ our light', to which all respond, 'Thanks be to God'. It is then placed on a stand in the sanctuary, originally near the lectern to give light to the deacon as he sings the Easter Proclamation, the *Exsultet*: 'Rejoice, heavenly powers!', a hymn of joy to 'the true Light, which lighteth every man that cometh into the world' (Jn 1:9). At one time deacons composed their own proclamation, chanting from a roll on which pictures were displayed upside-down so that they could be seen by the congregation as each sheet was thrown over the lectern.

The Vigil continues with the liturgy of the word, beginning with prophetic readings from the Old Testament, interspersed with responsorial psalms and prayers said standing, recalling the ancient way of praying. As the prayer after the last Old Testament reading ends, the altar candles are lighted, church bells ring out, veils (if any) are removed, and *Gloria in excelsis Deo*, 'Glory be to God on high', resounds in thanksgiving for the good news of salvation, heralded by the intoning of 'Alleluia, alleluia, alleluia!', before the reading of one of the Gospel accounts of the discovery of the empty tomb. If there are candidates to be baptized, this sacrament is administered after the chanting of the litany of the saints and the blessing of the font, into which the Easter Candle may be lowered and raised, signifying cleansing from sin and rising into new life. All renew their baptismal promises, standing with lighted candles as they make their profession of faith. They are then aspersed, sprinkled with holy water, to the singing of *Vidi aquam*: 'I saw water flowing', a time-honoured hymn based on Ezekiel's vision of water flowing from the right side of the house (Ez 47:1–2), prophetic of the water which issued from the wound of the crucified Christ.

The Vigil ends with the liturgy of the Eucharist, the people being dismissed after communion with words which are used at every Mass during the weeks which follow until Pentecost, 'Go in the peace of Christ, alleluia, alleluia', to which the response is, 'Thanks be to God, alleluia, alleluia'.

EASTER DAY   Although the Easter Vigil and the night commemoration of the resurrection of Christ accords with ancient tradition, for many congregations celebration of the greatest festival of the Christian year takes place on Sunday morning in churches adorned with easter lilies and other spring flowers which match white or gold vestments worn on that day. 'This is the day which the Lord hath made; we will rejoice and be glad in it' (Ps 118/117:24). Special hymns and anthems enhance the happiness of the occasion. 'Blessed be the God and father of our Lord Jesus Christ, which according to his abundant mercy hath begotten us again unto a lively hope by the resurrection of Jesus Christ from the dead' (1 P 1:3).

There were no witnesses to the resurrection: the guards at the tomb 'became as dead men' when an earthquake struck and an angel descended and rolled back the stone which sealed it (Mt 28:1–2). The gospel for the day is therefore one of the accounts of the discovery of the empty tomb, differing in detail but agreeing in the essential message: 'Christ is risen from the dead, and become the firstfruits of them that slept' (1 Cor 15:20).

Eastertide

As in early centuries, the fifty days from the Sunday of the Resurrection, the last day of the Easter Triduum, to evening prayer on Pentecost now constitute a season of uninterrupted rejoicing, foretaste of eternity when those who are called to 'the marriage supper of the Lamb' will pass the time in perpetual praise. The liturgical colour is white, symbol of happiness, and 'Alleluia', the song of the redeemed, resounds, recalling 'the voice of mighty thunderings, saying Alleluia: for the Lord God omnipotent reigneth' (Rv 19:6,9). The Paschal Candle, visible symbol of the risen Christ's presence, remains in the sanctuary. At Compline, the last office of the day, and on other occasions, according to custom, *Regina coeli laetare*: 'Queen of heaven, rejoice', the Eastertide anthem, is sung standing, in the early Church the usual posture for prayer at this season. A legend, current towards the end of the thirteenth century, attributes this anthem to Gregory the Great who, at the height of the epidemic which decimated the population of Rome in 590, ordered the icon of the Blessed Virgin, said to have been painted by St Luke, to be borne through the city in a penitential procession. As it was carried across the bridge over the Tiber, angels were heard singing the first three lines, calling upon Mary to rejoice because her son had risen. Gregory completed the quatrain with a fervent, '*Ora pro nobis Deum, Alleluia!*': 'Pray for us to God, Alleluia'. At that moment the Archangel Gabriel appeared above the mausoleum of the Emperor Hadrian and sheathed his sword, a sign that the plague was over. A chapel was built on the monument which was renamed Castel Sant' Angelo: 'Castle of the Holy Angel'.

In fact, the earliest known text of the anthem dates from about the end of the twelfth century, possibly based on the legend that the angel Gabriel appeared to Mary, sorrowing after the entombment of her son, and bade her rejoice, 'for the Lord has risen indeed!' The anthem was popularized by the Franciscans and included in the Divine Office.

THE EASTER OCTAVE   The eight days from Easter, counting inclusively, retain much of the distinctive character which they acquired from the fourth century onwards, especially after 389 when the Roman emperor declared the week a holiday so that the newly baptized should be given further instruction in the mysteries of the faith. As in the Roman rite, there is provision in Anglican and Episcopalian service books for a daily Eucharist with prefaces, sentences and lections appropriate to the appearances of the risen Christ. The *Book of Common Prayer*, in which the word 'octave' is avoided, recognizes Monday and Tuesday as special, possibly reflecting governmental reaction against the medieval multiplication of public holidays.

One of the gospel readings for this week relates Christ's appearance by the Sea of Tiberias when he revealed that he was no spirit but resurrected flesh and blood when he breakfasted with his disciples on bread and fish cooked on a charcoal fire. This was the source of the eucharistic symbolism in early Christian art in which a fish is shown on an altar-like table. A fish was also an arcane symbol for Christ because the initial letters of Greek *icthus*: 'fish', formed an acrostic interpreted as 'Jesus Christ, Son of God, Saviour'. In a third-century epitaph found in 1839 at Autun in Burgundy, Pectorius, a Christian, asked his friends and relations to remember him 'in the peace of the fish'.

LOW SUNDAY   The Second Sunday of Easter, the conclusion of the Octave, was known as Quasimodo Sunday because the Latin introit, or entrance song, began, *Quasi modo geniti infantes*: 'Like new-born babes' (1 P 2:2), a phrase appropriate to the newly baptized, known as *infantes*: 'babies', because they had been born again in the waters of baptism and become 'children of the Lord'. In Rome they assembled the previous evening in the basilica of St John Lateran and handed back the white robes which they had worn during the octave. The Sunday was therefore also known as *Domenica in albis deponendis*: 'Sunday after laying white robes aside'. Then they went to Mass at the church of San Pancrazio, dedicated to St Pancras, the fourth-century boy martyr, patron of those who kept contracts, witness to their determination to preserve their baptismal vows.

Low Sunday, the name by which the day is called in England, is not meant to contrast it with the 'high' celebration of Easter. The qualifying adjective is the anglicization of Latin *laudes*: 'praise', a reference to the sequence, *Laudes Salvatori*: 'Praise to the Saviour'.

A gospel reading appropriate to this octave Sunday is the account of the appearance of Christ eight days after his resurrection to Thomas, called Didymus, the Twin, who had been absent the previous Sunday and had refused to believe Christ's physical manifestation unless he could see the holes that the nails had made and had put his hand into his side. Christ, again entering the room where the disciples were assembled, invited Thomas to make the test, whereupon the apostle responded, 'My Lord and my God' (Jn 20:19–28). It is not stated that he actually touched Jesus but in art he is shown probing the wound in the side, the eponymous 'Doubting Thomas'.

GOOD SHEPHERD SUNDAY   A powerful image for a pastoral society was the description of the Lord God as the caring shepherd who, like the boy David, an Old Testament type of Christ, slew the lion and the bear to protect his flock (I S 17:34–7). Jesus said, 'I am the good shepherd', contrasting himself with the hireling who flees when the wolf attacks (Jn 10:11–18). In the *Book of Common Prayer*, 'the Second Sunday after Easter' ('Fourth Sunday of Easter' in the *Roman Missal*) is therefore known as 'Good Shepherd Sunday'. The epistle for that day, in which Christ is described as 'the Shepherd and Bishop of your souls' (1 P2:25 AV), provides the Protestant justification for a bishop's pastoral staff, or so it is said.

THE ASCENSION OF THE LORD   When Jesus taught in the synagogue at Capernaum in the early days of his ministry, he said to those puzzled by his statement, 'I have come down from heaven': 'What if you see the Son of man ascend to where he was before?' (Jn 6:62). At the last supper he told his disciples, 'I came from the Father and have come into the world and now I am leaving the world to go to the Father' (Jn 16:28). At the heart of the preaching of the apostles, pervading letters written to the first Christian communities, was the fact of the ascension of the risen Christ, 'his exaltation to the right hand of God'. The rudimentary creed, or early hymn, which Paul quoted in his letter to Timothy ended on the triumphant note that Christ was 'taken up in glory' (1 Tm 3:16). At that time the emphasis was on the theological meaning, not the manner of the ascension. Luke the Evangelist supplied two seemingly contradictory versions of the event, explained as consonant with the convention of expanding at a later stage a previously mentioned historical incident. The first, also paraphrased in the longer ending of the *Gospel of Mark* (Mk 16:19), stated that, apparently on the day of his resurrection, Jesus led his disciples as far as Bethany, a small village on the south-eastern slope of the Mount of Olives, where, 'as he blessed them, he withdrew from them and was carried up into heaven' (Lk 24:51). The second account also located the ascension on the Mount of Olives but at a short distance from Jerusalem, 'no more than a Sabbath walk' – the two thousand paces permitted by rabbinic law.

Towards the end of the fourth century, Poemenia, a noble Roman lady, built a church on the traditional site, the hillock known as the Imbomon (Ac 1:2–11). Early commentators disagreed as to the timing of the event which in Luke's second account happened after the apostles had seen Christ alive 'for forty days'. Some interpreted this as an idiom for 'a long time'; Eusebius, bishop of Caesarea, said that it equalled the three-and-a-half years duration of Jesus' public ministry; but the creed promulgated at the Council of Toledo (400) accepted the literal meaning of the phrase. This influenced the fixing of the festival forty days after Easter, the Thursday of the sixth week of Eastertide, whereas initially the ascension had been commemorated at Pentecost.

The biblical pre-Copernican universe depicted the earth as a flat surface with projecting mountains, sustained on pillars; below was Sheol, the place of departed spirits; above, where the stars shone, was the vault of the sky; and above that again, God's heavenly abode. An early representation of the clause in the creed affirmed by the First General Council of Nicaea (325), 'he ascended to the heavens', an ivory panel *c.*400, showed a youthful Christ leaving the Mount of Olives, welcomed by the hand of God which emerged from the sky, but this yielded to a convention more in accord with the old cosmology. Eleven apostles (or twelve if Paul, an anachronism, is included opposite Peter) are ranged around the Blessed Virgin, assumed to have been present because she prayed with the apostles (Ac I:14). They gaze sorrowfully upwards as a cloud, symbolic of the divine presence but mistaken in art for a real cloud, hides Christ from them. Two men in white apparel, assumed to be angels, address the apostles as 'Ye men of Galilee' (echoed in the antiphon for the festival, *Viri Galilee*) and with their gestures explain the cosmic meaning of the event: 'this same Jesus which is taken up from you into heaven, shall come in like manner as ye have seen him go into heaven'.

Ascension Day is therefore an occasion for joyful celebration. The refrain of the responsorial psalm is, 'God is gone up with a shout, the Lord with the sound of a trumpet', but this is the prelude to his return as 'a great king over all the earth' (Ps 47/46:4–7). Meanwhile, as stated in Cranmer's collect, derived from the Gregorian Sacramentary, the hope is that 'we may also in heart and mind thither ascend, and with him continually dwell'.

Before 1955 and the reforms initiated by the Second Vatican Council it was customary to interrupt the pentecostal season of rejoicing after Ascension Day and to resume fasting and abstinence during the octave (now suppressed). The Paschal Candle was extinguished (in some places hauled up to the roof to symbolize Christ's ascent!). It now remains in the sanctuary. As the apostles 'returned to Jerusalem with great joy', so too Christians continue for the next ten days to celebrate their Lord's resurrection and to pray for his return.

PENTECOST: WHITSUNDAY   In his discourse after supper, Jesus promised his sorrowing disciples that the Father would send in his name the Paraclete, a Greek word variously rendered as 'advocate' (in a lawsuit), 'helper', or, as in earlier English versions, 'comforter', because it would console them after his death. Jesus equated the term with the Holy Spirit (Jn 14:16, 26). Before he was taken up into heaven, he therefore told his followers to remain in Jerusalem because within a few days they would be baptized with the Holy Spirit. This happened on the morning of the Jewish festival of Pentecost when the disciples were assembled in a house, unnamed but traditionally the *cenaculum*: 'upper room', above the present building known as 'David's tomb', the site of an early Christian church.

Pentecost, once the name for the fifty-day season of Eastertide but now restricted to the festival-day itself, is named in English Whitsunday (late Old English *Hwita Sunnandaeg*: 'White Sunday'), recalling the white robes worn on that day by the newly-baptized. The Vigil Mass in the present Roman rite is reminiscent of the fact that until the twelfth century, except in cases of extreme urgency, Pentecost was, with Easter, one of the only two permitted occasions for baptism.

The number of disciples present when tongues as of fire separated and came to rest on the head of each one of them is not stated – 120 were assembled when Matthias was chosen by lot to replace Judas – but conventionally twelve apostles (or thirteen if Paul is included) are depicted. The presence of Mary, 'the mother of Jesus', who constantly prayed with the apostles is also assumed (Ac 1:14). Because of her exalted status, and because she represents the Church which came into being on that day, she occupies the central position.

Reception of the Holy Spirit caused the apostles 'to speak with other tongues', an ecstatic phenomenon known as glossolalia. Outside the house, attracted by the uproar, were many devout Jews who had come to end their days in Jerusalem, and pilgrims from the scattered communities of the *diaspora*. To their astonishment they heard words in the languages of the various countries where they lived. Attempts have been made to arrange the peoples listed into twelve groups corresponding to the signs of the zodiac then thought to govern the nations of the world, because it is evidently the intention of the writer to show that 'the mighty words of God' are to be preached to all mankind (Ac 2:1–11). Typologically the event is seen as the reversal of the linguistic confusion consequent upon man's impious attempt to build the Tower of Babel (Gn 11:1–9).

In the Jewish tradition, the festival of Pentecost, seven times seven days plus one, the fiftieth day, symbolized the closure of the period of harvest rejoicing. For Christians it represented the end of the old dispensation and the beginning of the new age, dominated by the Holy Spirit, which would culminate in the return of Christ after his gospel had been preached 'to the uttermost part of the earth' (Ac 1:8).

The liturgical colour for Pentecost Sunday is red, recalling the 'tongues of fire', the flames of the Holy Spirit. The responsorial psalm has the refrain, 'Send forth your spirit, O Lord, and renew the face of the earth' (Ps 103/102). Also sung is the hymn *Veni Sancte Spiritus*: 'Come, Holy Spirit', once attributed to Innocent III but now known to have been composed by his friend, Stephen Langton (*d.*1228), archbishop of Canterbury. The octave which followed this Sunday in the Roman rite was discontinued following the reforms of the Second Vatican Council. In the *Book of Common Prayer* the Monday and Tuesday after Whitsunday are Red Letter days, so called because days provided with a proper collect, epistle and gospel were marked in the calendar with red ink.

In the Jewish tradition the fiftieth day marked the completion of the period of harvest rejoicing. Pentecost, in the Christian tradition, is seen as the triumphant conclusion of the cycle of the seasons of the year which began with Advent and which will be resumed the next Advent. The Paschal Candle is placed in the baptistry and from it are lit the candles of the newly baptized, testimony of the association of their baptism with the Easter mystery.

Solemnities and Feasts
of the Lord

OME THIRTY-THREE TO THIRTY-FOUR Sundays, depending on the position of Easter and the number of Sundays in a given year, lie outside the Advent to Pentecost cycle. They constitute the General Season of the Year, or Ordinary Time, when in the main the focus is on Jesus' earthly ministry, his teaching and his miracles, beginning with his baptism, celebrated by a feast on the first Sunday which follows 6 January. The sequence is interrupted at Lent, is resumed after Pentecost, and concludes on the Sunday before Advent. Within this General Season are Solemnities and Feasts of the Lord, mostly celebrating the theological implications of his incarnation.

The Baptism of the Lord

In his *Antiquities of the Jews* (c.94) Flavius Josephus, the Jewish historian, described John the Baptist as a good man who urged his fellow Jews to live righteously and to be baptized for the purification of the body, 'when the soul had been already cleansed by justice'. A cross on the fragmentary sixth-century Greek-lettered mosaic map in the museum at Madaba, Jordan, marks the traditional site near Beth-'araba: 'town on the ford', a crossing-point on the River Jordan, where John saw Jesus coming towards him and proclaimed, 'Behold the Lamb of God who takes away the sin of the world' (Jn 1:29).

That Jesus, who was sinless, should have submitted to John's 'baptism of repentance for the remission of sins', obviously perplexed the writer of the *Gospel of Matthew*. To the succinct factual statement derived from the *Gospel of Mark* he therefore added that, when John remonstrated, saying that it was he who should be baptized by one greater than he, Jesus insisted that it was necessary for him to accept John's baptism 'to fulfil all righteousness'. All four Gospels agree as to the transcendental meaning of what then happened: the descent on Jesus of the Holy Spirit, 'like a dove',

73

Hebrew symbol of divine authority; and the voice which came from heaven, proclaiming, 'This is my beloved Son'.

In the Eastern tradition Jesus' baptism, a theophany, or manifestation of his divinity; his revelation of himself to the Wise Men; and the miracle which he performed at Cana – all were commemorated on Epiphany, 6 January in the Julian calendar, a date which was also the symbolic festival of his birth. As Jesus' nativity was celebrated in the West on 25 December, Epiphany there emphasized the visitation of the Wise Men, thus avoiding duplication, the account of his baptism becoming the gospel for the octave day of 6 January. In the revised Roman calendar of 1969 the feast of the Baptism of the Lord was assigned to the Sunday following 6 January, or to the next day should that Sunday be Epiphany, a practice now followed by other Churches. The story of the wedding feast at Cana is the gospel for the second Sunday after Epiphany in one of the cycle of readings. The commemoration of Jesus' baptism, the beginning of his public ministry, is thus the point of transition from Christmastide to the General Season of the Year.

The Presentation of the Lord

A primitive pagan fertility rite, the sacrifice of a first-born, was transformed by the spiritual leaders of Israel into the consecration of an eldest son to the service of the Lord God who abhorred the slaughter of children. This was also a perpetual reminder of his mercy when the avenging angel spared first-born males of the Israelites on the night of their escape from Egypt. In course of time, Levites, descendants of Levi, one of Jacob's sons, who ministered in the sanctuary, would perform the Temple service required of the child in return for the redemptive payment of five shekels of silver. Obedient to the Law of Moses, Joseph and Mary carried the infant Jesus to the Temple to be presented to the Lord. It is not stated that they paid the ritual tax, presumably because, like Samuel, who was dedicated by Hannah and Elkhana (the typological parallel), Jesus was from the first moment of his earthly life consecrated to his Father's service.

The presentation of Jesus also fulfilled Malachi's messianic prophecy, 'And suddenly the Lord whom you seek will come to his Temple' (MI 3:1). Simeon, 'an upright and devout man', to whom it had been revealed that he would not die until he had seen 'the Christ of the Lord', like a rabbi took Jesus in his arms and intoned the canticle known by the opening Latin words as *Nunc dimittis*: 'Now lettest thou thy servant depart in peace, for mine eyes have seen thy salvation'. Anna, an aged prophetess who had spent her long widowhood in the Temple, fasting and praying, 'began to praise God and spoke of the child to all who looked forward to the deliverance of Israel' (Lk 2:21–38).

This recognition of Jesus as Messiah coincided with Mary's compliance with an obligation placed on Jewish women, who were held to be unclean and forbidden to touch any holy object for seven days after the birth of a male child. After a further thirty three days, during which their blood was thought to cleanse itself, they were required, for their purification, to bring to the sanctuary a pigeon or a dove as a 'sin offering', and a year-old lamb for a 'burnt offering'. As Mary was poor, she availed herself of the clause which permitted the substitution for the lamb of a pair of turtle-doves or two young pigeons. Why Mary, who was sinless, needed purification troubled medieval theologians, but it was explained that, in her piety, she was always obedient to the Law.

These two events thus took place forty days after Jesus' birth, celebrated in the East on 14 February in the Julian calendar, forty days after Epiphany. In Jerusalem the festival was known by the Greek word *apantē* or *apantēsis*: 'meeting', in classical times used for the reception of an emperor, or his representative, when he was met by citizens who strewed flowers and greenery in his path, and was then escorted by lamp-bearers to their city. It would therefore be reasonable to assume that, as a Christianization of this custom, a procession would go out from Jerusalem to meet another coming from Bethlehem, in which, as in Palm Sunday processions, a bishop would represent the Lord. This is borne out by the statement by Cyril of Skythopolis, a sixth-century hagiographer, that Ikelia, a pious lady who had settled in the Holy Land about the middle of the previous century, advocated the use of wax candles for the procession of 'the meeting of the Lord'. This was more than a re-enactment of a past event: it had an eschatological meaning, recalling the Wise Virgins of the parable (Mt 25:1–13) who had their lamps ready trimmed to meet the Bridegroom (Christ) on his Second Coming.

A decree of the Emperor Justinian in 542 shows that when the feast was earlier introduced in Constantinople it was celebrated on 2 February, forty days after 25 December, the Western date for the festival of the Nativity of Jesus. This was also the date on which Sergius I (687–701) ordered that a procession should leave St Hadrian's church in the Forum and that the people should assemble in Santa Maria Maggiore (where, incidentally, the earliest Western depictions of the Presentation and

Purification are to be found) on 'St Symeon's day which the Greeks call Ypapanti'.

From the time of the Emperor Charlemagne onwards, corresponding to the devotion paid to Mary, the festival was known as the 'Purification of Saint Mary the Virgin', a title which passed, by way of the Sarum Missal, into the *First Prayer Book of Edward VI* (1549); but in 1662 this was changed to 'The Presentation of Christ in the Temple, commonly called, The Purification of Saint Mary the Virgin'. It is now a feast of the Lord.

Candlemas, the traditional name, derives from the candlelight procession in church, recalling Simeon's words, 'A light to lighten the Gentiles', which seems to have become popular in the eleventh century. Suppressed in England at the time of the Reformation, it was revived in the late nineteenth century, although frowned upon in 'The Lambeth Opinion', delivered in 1899 at Lambeth Palace by the archbishops of Canterbury and York. In the Catholic tradition, a procession forms before the Mass; candles are lighted and blessed; and the antiphon, 'Christ is the light of nations', based on Simeon's canticle, is sung. Although the celebrant's acclamation, 'Let us go in peace to meet the Lord', refers to meeting him in the Eucharist, it also recalls the remote origin of the feast when the Lord was met and escorted to his Temple.

The Annunciation of the Lord

The creed, or formula of belief, affirmed at the Council of Nicaea (325) and at the First General Council of Constantinople (381), recited by all Christians, states: 'For us men and for our salvation he came down from heaven: by the power of the Holy Spirit he became incarnate from the Virgin Mary, and was made man.' This festival, derived from the narrative in the *Gospel of Luke*, celebrates the way in which this came about. God sent the angel Gabriel to Mary, a virgin of a town in Galilee called Nazareth, to announce that she would bear a son whom she would name Jesus. He explained that the Holy Spirit would come upon her and that power of the Most High would cover her with its shadow, the cloud which in the scriptures symbolizes God's presence. At first fearful, Mary accepted her destiny, saying, 'Behold the handmaid of the Lord'. It is believed that at that moment the Son of God took flesh in her womb (Lk 1:26–38).

This episode is the one most frequently represented in the life of the Virgin in art. Mary is usually shown in a room in a house at Nazareth. (A large basilica, the church of the Annunciation, begun in 1954, stands on the site of the crusaders' church built where it was believed her home stood.) She is sometimes shown with a distaff, an Eastern convention, weaving the veil of the Temple which will be rent in twain at the crucifixion, because she is the new Eve, reversing the disobedience of the first woman who was condemned to spin when she and Adam were expelled from Paradise. In Western art she is usually seated, praying or reading the prophetic words, 'Behold a virgin shall conceive. . . .'. Her hands shown crossed over her breast reveal that she has given her assent to Gabriel's message.

A feast in honour of the Annunciation may have been instituted soon after 400 when a church was built in Nazareth in commemoration of the event, but the first authentic mention of one in the West was made at the Council of Toledo (656). In Rome it was one of the feasts on which St Sergius I (687–701) ordered a solemn procession. As explained earlier (Origins, p.21), the date of the festival, 25 March, the vernal equinox in the Julian calendar, symbolized both the creation of the universe and the new creation in Christ. It was also the day when the first man was formed and thus appropriately the day of the incarnation of the Second Adam who was born nine months later on 25 December, the feast of his nativity.

In England, the feast of the Annunciation is traditionally 'Lady Day' ('lady' being the genitive form in Old English). A feast of the universal Church, and since 1969 a feast of the Lord, it is transferred should it fall on a Sunday.

The Most Holy Trinity: Trinity Sunday

Central to the Christian faith, distinguishing it from other monotheistic traditions, is the concept of God as one divine substance which comprises three distinct and co-equal persons: Father, Son and Holy Spirit, 'three in one and one in three'. To express this mystery, a truth divinely revealed but not contrary to reason, Tertullian (c.160–c.225) used the word *trinitas*, the Latin form of the Greek *trías*: 'triad', not found in Scripture but implicit in early benedictional, baptismal and credal statements.

How to explain this mystery of the Triune God with doctrinal precision, a task which gave rise to many heresies, is illustrated by the legend related of St Augustine of Hippo, author of the philosophical treatise *On the Trinity* in fifteen books. On the sea shore he saw a child with a shell trying to empty the ocean into a hole in the sand. When he remarked on the impossibility of the task, the child replied that it was no more difficult than Augustine's attempt to define the Trinity. The classic definition was given in the creed promulgated by the First General Council of Nicaea (325): 'We believe in the Holy Spirit, the Lord and Giver of Life, who proceeds from the Father, who together with the Father and Son is worshipped and glorified.' (The words 'and the Son', not accepted by the Orthodox Church, were added after 'from the Father' by the Third General Council of Toledo in 589.)

Offices in honour of the Holy Trinity were composed in certain monasteries from the late seventh century onwards. There were also votive Masses, said at the discretion, or 'choice' (Latin *votum*), of the priest, notable examples being that composed *c*.800 by Alcuin, the renowned scholar, born and educated in York, who became adviser on liturgical matters to the Emperor Charlemagne; and the Office for the Mass by Stephen, bishop of Liège from 903–20. Most influential was the Mass of the Holy Trinity, celebrated in the eleventh century in the Benedictine monastery at Cluny, Burgundy and spreading from there to daughter-houses in other parts of France and in Spain. Special merit was acquired by attendance at this Mass. (In the medieval Spanish epic, the eponymous hero, Ruy Díaz de Vivar, known as El Cid, hears the Mass of the Holy Trinity before making an incursion into Moorish territory.)

Although tolerating these local celebrations, successive popes, following the lead given by Alexander II (1061–73), resisted requests for a fixed day in the calendar for a Trinitarian feast, on the grounds that the Trinity was honoured daily when *Gloria Patri*, the ascription of praise, 'Glory be to the Father and to the Son and to the Holy Spirit', concluded a psalm. The need to combat Unitarian heresies, notably those propounded by Albigensians and Waldensians, 'the poor men of Lyons', followers of Peter Valdes (*d.c.*1205–18), and pressure from Cistercians who had instituted a Trinitarian Mass in 1271 at Cîteaux, their mother-house, caused John XXII, in 1334 at Avignon, to consent to a universal feast on the first Sunday after Pentecost, conveniently a Sunday without an appointed Mass, following the commemoration of the descent of the Holy Spirit, thus completing the cycle honouring all three Persons.

Devotion to the Trinity was introduced in England after the Norman Conquest in 1066. It was intensified after St Thomas Becket, consecrated archbishop on 3 June 1162, the octave of Pentecost, in the Trinity Chapel of Canterbury Cathedral (later destroyed by fire), ordered that the Most Holy Trinity should be honoured on that day throughout his province to commemorate his elevation. The rededication in 1542 of the church of the monastery of St Augustine in Bristol as the cathedral of The Most Holy and

Undivided Trinity, and foundations such as Trinity College, Cambridge show that ascription to the Holy Trinity was seen by the Reformers in England as a means of countering the excessive veneration of saints. Similar dedications of some 230 churches built in England in the nineteenth century illustrate the avoidance of saints' names by the Evangelical party in the Church of England.

Following the ancient usage of Sarum, the *Book of Common Prayer* numbers Sundays until Advent as 'after Trinity', as do some Lutheran Churches. Roman, Episcopalian and modern Anglican calendars make Pentecost the starting-point.

Corpus Christi: The Body and Blood of Christ. Thanksgiving for the institution of Holy Communion

Until the eleventh century it was generally accepted, without undue speculation as to the effect of the change on the eucharistic elements, that at the consecration the bread and the wine became the body and blood of Christ. Then Berengarius (*c.*1010–88), head of the school of St Martin in his native Tours, sparked off a theological debate which was concluded for the time being when St Thomas Aquinas (*c.*1225–74), using categories derived from Aristotelian philosophy, produced the classic explanation that the 'substances', the outward appearances of the bread and wine, are transformed into the 'essence', the unchanging reality of Christ, that is they are 'transubstantiated', a word which had gained currency after its use in a letter (1202) written by Innocent III to John, a former archbishop of Tours, a poet and one of the builders of Le Mans cathedral.

Meanwhile, to combat the heresies of Cathari and Albigensians in the south of France and the errors of the followers of the mystic, Joachim of Fiore (*c.*1132–1202), in 1215 the Fourth General Lateran Council, in the course of insisting that the consecration could only be performed by a properly ordained priest, declared dogmatically that Christ's body and blood 'are truly contained in the sacrament of the altar under the appearances of bread and wine, the bread being transubstantiated into the body by the divine power and the wine into the blood'. This confirmed a devotion practised in certain monastic communities whereby, when the celebrant at Mass 'elevated', lifted up, the bread (elevation of the chalice was a later development), the congregation knelt or prostrated themselves in adoration

79

of Christ's presence. It was also the custom for the consecrated host to be 'reserved', placed in a pyx, a receptacle usually hung over the altar, a lamp being kept burning nearby to indicate the corporal presence of Christ.

These practices afforded great spiritual comfort, and often moments of ecstasy to many in the Meuse valley, where there was a religious revival, when they witnessed the elevation, or knelt in prayer before the reserved sacrament. A manifestation of this renewed spirituality was the formation of contemplative and philanthropic brotherhoods and sisterhoods, the Beghards and Beguines who apparently derived their titles from Lambert (*d.*1177), nicknamed *le Bègue*: 'the stammerer', who preached in Liège, advocating renunciation of worldly wealth and status.

Aware of these developments, and in general terms of the debate over transubstantiation, was Juliana (1192–1258), an orphan from a wealthy family in the village of Rétinne, close to Liège, who at the age of sixteen made her profession as a nun in the convent of the Canonesses Regular (Augustinians) in nearby Mont-Cornillon. At prayer in the convent chapel before the Blessed Sacrament, she was favoured *c.*1208 with a vision in which she saw a full moon, its beauty marred by a dark shadow. She later understood that the moon represented the liturgical year (in some versions the Church) and that the blemish on its surface revealed the absence of a festival in honour of the body of Christ. To this cause she dedicated her life, receiving, after her election as prioress in 1222, the support of the Dominican House of Studies in Liège and of Robert de Thourote, the bishop, who in 1246 gave permission for the feast to be celebrated in his diocese.

Juliana, faced by a revolt of her nuns, who resented her attempt at reform, and victim of a civil conflict to control the funds of the leper hospital, after much suffering ended her days (26 April 1252) as a recluse with the Beguines at Saint-Fevillen, Fosse, near Namur. Her campaign for the festival was taken up by the Blessed Eve, a recluse of the church, of Saint-Martin (*c.*1221–*c.*64) to whom she had confided her visions. Eve was rewarded when Jacques Pantaléon, who as archdeacon of Liège had supported Juliana, was elevated to the papacy as Urban IV, and on 8 September 1264 declared universal the feast of Corpus Christi. The Mass and Office for the day is said to have been composed by St Thomas Aquinas, then teaching at Orvieto.

A tradition relating to the foundation of Orvieto cathedral, the subject of one of Raphael's frescoes for the Stanza della Segnatura, one of the sets of papal rooms in the Vatican, attributes Urban's authorization of the feast to a miracle related to him when he visited Orvieto. A German priest who had grave doubts about the doctrine of Transubstantiation, when on a pilgrimage to Rome was celebrating Mass at the Church of Santa Christina at Bolsena when he accidentally spilled some of the wine and covered it with a corporal, the linen cloth which symbolizes the winding sheet in which Joseph of Arimathea wrapped the body of Christ. He later discovered that the red spots had taken the shape of the Host. The report of this miracle convinced Urban that the feast was divinely ordained and that a cathedral should be built at Orvieto to house the relic; it is now contained in a fine silver shrine in the Capella del Corporale (Chapel of the Corporal).

After Urban's death in 1264 the feast seems to have been neglected: Clement V, at the Council of Vienne (1311–12), found it necessary to confirm Urban's bull, and John XXII in 1317 again had to emphasize its importance. Nevertheless, in Provence and the Catalan-speaking areas of Barcelona and Valencia the day provided the occasion for the Blessed Sacrament to be carried through the city, accompanied by a carnival-like procession. In Spain this custom, first noted in Cologne in 1212, gave rise to a new genre of one-act allegorical plays, performed in movable carts, glorifying the Eucharist.

It is necessary to understand the origin of the festival and the underlying theological reason for it because, for centuries, the doctrine of Transubstantiation has divided Western Christendom. Martin Luther was prepared to accept that the bread and wine subsisted together with Christ's body and blood but Zwingli (1484–1531), the Swiss reformer, rejected this concept altogether. At its thirteenth session in 1551, the Council of Trent reaffirmed that 'the outward appearances of bread and wine remain but a complete change of substance into the Body and Blood of Christ takes place at the Eucharist'. In England, the Forty-Two Articles (1553), mostly the work of Thomas Cranmer, stated unequivocally that 'Transubstantiation (or the change of the substance of Bread and Wine) . . . cannot be proved by Holy Writ; but is repugnant to the plain words of Scripture, overthroweth the nature of the sacrament and hath given occasion to many superstitions.'

Moderate English churchmen, after witnessing the horrors attendant upon the restoration of the Catholic faith under Queen Mary (1553–58) and the equally bloody reaction when Protestantism regained the ascendant, calmed their consciences with a formula, attributed to Queen Elizabeth I, which could be interpreted in favour of either orthodoxy:

> *His was the word that spake it;*
> *He took the bread and brake it:*

> And what that Word did make it,
> I do believe and take it.

Mercifully, a new philosophical approach to religious symbolism and to the old scholastic categories now provides the way forward to the reconciliation of hitherto rival eucharistic doctrines and favours a diversity of practice within the Anglican Communion.

It is now possible for the *Prayer Book* of the American Episcopal Church to include a revised version of the collect thought to have been composed by St Thomas Aquinas for the feast and for those using the *Alternative Service Book* to observe 'a day of Thanksgiving for the Institution of Holy Communion' on the Thursday after Trinity Sunday, coinciding with 'The Body and Blood of Christ' in the *Roman Missal*. In the Roman calendar this festival may be held on the Sunday after Trinity Sunday if the Thursday is not a public holiday.

The Sacred Heart of Jesus

Ancient physiology located the emotions in various bodily organs, the heart being the seat of love. Devotion to the corporal heart of Jesus, symbol of his abiding love, was a feature of the spiritual life of many medieval mystics but the modern liturgical cult of the Sacred Heart of Jesus, a devotion of the Roman Catholic Church, originated in France in the seventeenth century.

It was first promoted by St John Eudes (1601–80) who came from Ri in Normandy. Educated at the Jesuit college at Caen, he joined the Congregation of the Oratory (Oratorians) in 1623 and, after caring for victims of a plague, devoted himself to the reclamation of prostitutes. In 1643 he founded the Congregation of Jesus and Mary, composed of secular clergy who wore a badge depicting the hearts of Jesus and Mary. After some opposition, he obtained permission to celebrate on 31 August 1670, in the seminary chapel, the Mass of the Sacred Heart, for which he had composed texts. Although some other French dioceses permitted the feast, it did not achieve widespread popularity because of personal opposition to Eudes.

More effective in the long term were the visions and influence of St Margaret-Mary Alacoque (1647–90), of the convent at Paray-le-Monial in Burgundy, of the Order of the Visitation of the Blessed Virgin Mary (Visitandines), a contemplative Order founded in 1610 by St Francis de Sales and St Jeanne Frances de Chantal. While engaged on menial tasks in the convent infirmary, humiliated because she was slow and clumsy, she was consoled by the feeling that Christ was constantly at her side. On 27

December 1673, at prayer before the Blessed Sacrament, she heard the Lord inviting her to lean on his bosom, as did St John, 'the Beloved Disciple', whose feast-day it was. In a series of visions, spread over eighteen months and culminating on the octave of Corpus Christi, she was confirmed in the knowledge that she had been chosen to spread the devotion to Christ's heart, testimony of his love, and that, in expiation of man's indifference to his sufferings, a feast should be instituted on the day of her final vision.

This did not come about without considerable opposition, first from Margaret-Mary's superior, who refused to believe her visions unless a nun were cured of a serious illness, which in fact happened. Support came from Claude La Colombière, a Jesuit and spiritual director at the convent, who convinced the sisters that the visions were not the delusions of a sickly woman. In contrast, Jansenists, followers of Cornelius Otto Jansen (1585–1638), opposed the institution of the feast on the grounds that devotion to Jesus' physical heart separated his humanity from his divinity. In 1697 and again in 1729 the Congregation of Sacred Rites refused to sanction the feast, but Clement XIII in 1765 gave permission for a Mass and Office in certain churches, and this was later extended to other dioceses. So popular was the devotion – statues with a wounded heart, encircled by a crown of thorns and radiating light, were installed in churches and vigils held on the first Friday of each month, as requested in Margaret-Mary's vision – that in 1856 Pius IX made the feast universal, fixed on the Friday after the second Sunday after Pentecost. The famous Sacré-Coeur (consecrated in 1919) on top of the Butte Montmartre in Paris, was built in fulfilment of a vow taken after the defeat of the French by the Prussians in 1870.

During the jubilee year of 1900, Leo XIII solemnly consecrated mankind to the Sacred Heart of Jesus, and Pius XII, in his Encyclical Letter (1956), clarified the theological foundation for devotion to 'the Heart of the divine Redeemer . . . the natural sign and symbol of his boundless charity for the human race . . .'. The present Mass in the *Roman Missal*, although mentioning the need for reparation for man's rejection of Christ's love, as Margaret-Mary was told in her vision, now emphasizes the positive response to the gifts of love, 'for the love of the Lord is everlasting'.

The Transfiguration of the Lord

'When we told you about the power and coming of our Lord Jesus Christ, we were not slavishly repeating cleverly invented myths; no, we had seen his majesty with our own eyes. He was honoured and glorified by God the

Father, when a voice came to him from the transcendent Glory, "This is my Son, the Beloved, he enjoys my favour". We ourselves heard this voice from heaven, when we were with him on the holy mountain' (2 P I:16–18).

This testimony, preserved in a letter of unknown authorship but attributed to 'Simon Peter, servant and apostle of Jesus Christ', referred to the event recounted in the three synoptic Gospels (which differ as to detail but agree in essentials) when, as Jesus prayed, he was transformed, or 'transfigured'. The appearance of his countenance was altered; his face shone like the sun; and his garments became as white as light. Moses, whose face shone on Mount Sinai when in the presence of the Lord God, and Elijah, to whom God spoke in a still small voice, appeared alongside him. A cloud, the *shekinah*, symbolizing the presence of God, like the cloud which received Jesus at his Ascension, overshadowed them and, as at Jesus' baptism, a voice from heaven was heard to say, 'This is my beloved son' (Mt 17:1–13; Mk 9:2–13; Lk 9:28–36).

The 'high mountain' to which Jesus led Peter, James and his brother John is now thought to be Mount Hermon, north of Caesarea Philippi, where six days before Peter had acknowledged Jesus as Messiah, the Son of the living God (Mt 16:16), but in 333 an unknown pilgrim from Bordeaux was told that it was a mound on the Mount of Olives. Not long afterwards, when St Jerome lived as a hermit in the Syrian desert, Mount Tabor, in the plain of Esdraelon, was favoured. In 326 St Helena, mother of Constantine the Great, built a basilica there and in the sixth century three churches were erected on the spot, commemorating the three tents, or tabernacles, which Peter offered to make, one for Jesus, and one each for Moses and Elijah, representing the Law and the Prophets, who were seen alongside him, linking the Transfiguration with the end of time because it was believed that the appearance of Moses and Elijah would herald the Second Coming of Christ.

A festival, possibly originating in the dedication of the earliest church, was observed in some Eastern Churches in the sixth century and by the eighth century, when St John of Damascus composed verses celebrating the day, it had become one of the twelve great festivals of the Orthodox calendar. Because it was calculated that the Transfiguration happened forty days before the crucifixion, commemorated on the feast of the Exaltation (now Triumph) of the Cross on 13 September, the festival was fixed on 6 August. It was observed in parts of the West, but did not become widely popular until the time of Peter the Venerable (*c*.1092–1156), eighth abbot of the monastery of Cluny, who composed an Office and a Mass for the festival and ordered it to be observed in all Cluniac houses. It nevertheless continued to be celebrated locally, mostly in Benedictine and Augustinian communities.

Institution as a feast of the universal Church came as the result of the crusade of Callistus III (1455–58) against the Turks. On 22 July 1456, St Mary Magdalene's day, a popular army recruited by St John of Capistrano, a Franciscan whom he had deputed to combat heresies preached by the followers of John Huss (c.1372–1415), assisted János Hunyadi, the Hungarian general, to rout the forces of Mohamet II and raise the siege of Belgrade. In August of the following year the Turkish fleet was defeated off Lesbos, a victory seen as granted by God. The monastic date, 6 August, was therefore adopted for the celebration of the Transfiguration of the Lord.

The Triumph of the Cross

The origin of this festival may be traced to an event on 13/14 September 335, when bishops assembled in Jerusalem for *Encaenia*: the 'dedication' of the basilica built by order of the Emperor Constantine which enclosed the Martyrium, the supposed site of the crucifixion on Golgotha. By the end of the century, what was intended as a celebration of thirty years of Constantine's reign, and his glorification of the holy places, had become an annual eight-day festival, ranking in liturgical splendour with Epiphany and Easter. The model was Solomon's dedication of the Temple (2 Ch 7:7–9), but it was later believed that originally the date had been chosen to coincide with the anniversary of the discovery of the remains of the cross during excavations on the site of the Temple of Venus. On 14 September, the second day of the festival, a relic of the cross, enshrined in a silver-gilt casket, was therefore displayed for veneration in the Martyrium.

The relic was carried off in 614 when forces of the Persian king Chroesröes (Khrosrow III) occupied Jerusalem; but it was recovered and returned there after Emperor Heraclius III (575–640) on 21 March 629 defeated the Persians on the banks of the Danube. On 14 September 633 the relic, taken to Constantinople for safekeeping, was carried in solemn procession to the Church of the Holy Wisdom (Sancta Sophia) and raised triumphantly on high for all to adore, recalling Christ's words, 'And I, if I be lifted up from the earth, will draw all men unto me' (Jn 12:32). This is the origin of the Orthodox festival of the Elevation of the Venerable Cross, one of the twelve great feasts of the year. Its introduction in the West, where it later became known as 'The Exaltation of the Cross' or 'Holy Cross Day', is attributed to Pope St Sergius I (687–701), who placed a relic of the cross for adoration on that day in the then Church of St Salvator, now known as the Lateran Basilica. It was retained in the *Book of Common Prayer* and is included in the *Prayer Book* of the American Episcopal Church but not in the *Alternative Service Book*.

Our Lord Jesus Christ, Universal King

To the 'one like the Son of man', whom Daniel saw in his vision, was given 'dominion, and glory, and a kingdom, that all people, nations and languages should serve him: his dominion is an everlasting dominion, which shall not pass away, and his kingdom that which shall not be destroyed' (Dn 7:14). In early credal statements, and in the creed promulgated by the First General Council of Constantinople (381), 'To his kingdom there will be no end' was declared to be an article of faith. Centuries later, Paul VI (1963–78) in his 'Solemn profession', made at the close of the 'year of faith' (1967–68) which he had called to commemorate the nineteenth centenary of the martyrdom of the apostles Peter and Paul, reiterated this clause and re-asserted, as essential to the faith, belief in the eternal kingship of Christ.

Already on 11 December 1925, towards the end of the Holy Year, the Jubilee 'year of remission' when indulgences are granted on certain conditions to those who pass through the Holy Door in the façade of St Peter's, Rome, Pius XI (1922–39) had instituted a feast in honour of Christ the King, to be kept on the Sunday before All Saints' Day (1 November). He explained in his encyclical letter *Quas Primas* that Christ's kingship gave him eternal dominion over man's spiritual life and social well-being and stressed the need to combat atheism and the secularization of human values. In 1970 the festival was transferred to the last Sunday in Ordinary Time, a triumphant conclusion to the calendar year before it begins anew at Advent when the faithful look forward to Christ's return when 'the Lord shall reign for ever' (Ps 146/145:10).

Although no provision for this festival is made in the *Alternative Service Book*, it is kept in many Anglican churches. In English popular usage the day, the 'Fifth Sunday before Christmas', or 'the Sunday next before Advent', is 'Stir up Sunday', a reminder to prepare the ingredients for Christmas pudding, because the collect in the *Book of Common Prayer* begins, 'Stir up, we beseech thee, O Lord, the wills of thy faithful people'! There is some affinity with the spirit of the Catholic festival in the epistle which quotes Jeremiah's prophecy, 'a king shall reign and prosper, and shall execute judgment and justice in the earth' (Jr 23:5).

Festivals of the Blessed Virgin Mary

ORSHIP, FOR WHICH THE THEOLOGICAL NAME is 'latria', a Latinization of the Greek *latreía*: 'service', is due to God alone. Reverence paid to angels and saints is 'dulia' (Greek *douleía*), the equivalent of 'veneration'. The Blessed Virgin Mary ranks with the saints but her unique role in God's plan of salvation entitles her to the higher degree of praise which Albert the Great (*c.*1200–80), the Dominican philosopher, and St Bonaventure (*c.*1217–74), among others, described as 'hyperdulia': 'more than veneration'. The incarnation of the Saviour depended on Mary's freely-given consent, 'Let it happen to me as you have said', her response to the message of the angel Gabriel. This is the reason why, as predicted, all generations call her blessed and why the numerous days of the year on which she is venerated, ranking next in importance to those dedicated to her son, take precedence over festivities of other saints.

As early as the mid-second century, St Justin Martyr described Mary as 'the New Eve' who, through her humble compliance with the will of God, countered the disobedience of the first mother of mankind. Her special status, the prime source of devotion to her person, was confirmed at the Council of Ephesus (431) when, in recognition of the fact that she bore Jesus Christ, one person but of two natures, human and divine, she was accorded the Greek title, *Theotókos*: 'God bearer', which in popular Latin usage became *Mater Dei*: 'Mother of God', although she was not so styled in Western conciliar documents until the Second Vatican Council (1962–65).

The liturgical cult of Mary originated in the East. A fragmentary mid-fourth-century papyrus from that region contains lines of a prayer of supplication to the Mother of God and there St Ephraem the Syrian (*c.*306–73) wrote hymns in her praise. There also were the first churches to be dedicated to her, their dates of consecration in many cases determining the timing of festivals associated with her personally, or with her and her son.

The earliest of these was the Purification (2 February), followed by the Dormition (15 August), the Annunciation (25 March), and, towards the end of the seventh century, the Birth of Mary (8 September). According to the *Liber Pontificalis*: 'Book of the Pontiffs', a collection of papal biographies, Sergius I (687–701), born in Palermo of Syrian parentage, ordered the litany to be recited in penitential processions on these four festivals which, possibly influenced by the devotions of the substantial Greek colony, by his time had been adopted in Rome. Until the fourteenth century these continued to be the principal Marian festivals in the West.

Meanwhile, encouraged by spiritual writers and religious Orders, devotion to Mary as charitable mother and protector was widespread. The month of May, originally named after the Roman goddess Maia, was dedicated to her. St Peter Damian (1107–72) promoted Saturday as Mary's day, thus extending the usual Friday fast and honouring her firm faith while her son lay in the tomb. Of monastic origin also was the Little Office of Our Lady, a form of daily prayer recited in choir as part of communal worship, or used for private devotion. In the later Middle Ages the text was set out in beautifully illuminated manuscript Books of Hours, adorned with decorated margins and small pictures. After the invention of printing, these were illustrated with woodcuts. From the Little Office was derived the Angelic Salutation, *Ave Maria*: 'Hail Mary', the most familiar of all prayers addressed to her. In the thirteenth century, Franciscan friars popularized the Angelus, the prayer commemorating the Annunciation and the Incarnation of Christ.

Although Benedict XIV (1740–58), the witty and scholarly pope, wished to restrict the number of Marian feasts, it has been calculated that by the twentieth century, spread over the world they numbered almost a thousand, many of local or monastic observance. Agreed conclusions as to the place of Mary in Christian teaching, discussed at the Second Vatican Council, were incorporated in the last chapter of the dogmatic constitution *Lumen Gentium* (1964). This was followed by Paul VI's Apostolic Exhortation *Marialis Cultus* (1974), which set out 'the principles for the right ordering and development of devotion to the Blessed Virgin'. Reform of the Marian calendar was therefore inevitable.

A distinction is now made between those feasts in which she was intimately involved but which were properly festivals of the Lord. Thirteen, exclusively hers and of universal application, are set out below, classified respectively as solemnities and obligatory and optional memorials. There is also provision, in certain circumstances, for festivals of provincial importance, a notable example being the feast of Our Lady of Guadalupe (12 December), whom Pius XI (1922–39) named patroness of All the Americas. It commemorates the appearance in December 1531 at the shrine of Guadalupe, on Tepeyac Hill outside Mexico City, to Juan Diego, an Indian, of the dark-featured Virgin to whom the indigenous population pay special veneration.

In the sixteenth century, Protestant reformers accepted scripturally-based teaching about Mary, praised her for her humility and extolled her as an example of womanhood, but rejected her power of intercession, maintaining that God could be approached only through Christ. Nevertheless they retained those festivals which had biblical authentication, notably the Annunciation and the Purification, which were included in the table of feasts in the *Book of Common Prayer* and which were also adopted in Prayer Books of various Churches of the Anglican Communion. Of recent years greater latitude has been permitted and, as will be noted below, it is now possible for those who favour the Catholic tradition to observe many, if not all, the Marian festivals in the *Roman Missal*.

Solemnity of Holy Mary, Mother of God

Manuscripts of the Gradual, the set of antiphons sung at the steps of the altar, attest that 1 January, the octave of the feast of the Nativity of Christ, was observed at one time as 'Anniversary of Mary'. In Rome this festival was associated with the church of Sancta Maria Antiqua, on the slopes of the Palatine Hill, built on the site of an earlier foundation by John VII (705–7), Greek by birth, who styled himself 'Servant of the Blessed Virgin'. This church, frequented by the Greek colony and by expatriate monks who had fled from Constantinople during the iconoclast, or anti-image controversy, was adorned with Byzantine-style murals in which Mary was exalted and was an influential centre for the diffusion of Marian devotion.

Later, although Mary was mentioned in the proper of the Mass and in the Divine Office, the day lost much of its Marian emphasis because, as Jesus was circumcised 'when the eighth day came', the octave became the Feast of the Circumcision, as it still is in many Churches. In 1969 it was restored in the Roman calendar as a celebration of Mary's divine motherhood, the theme of the Mass being based on St Paul's words, 'When the appointed time came, God sent his son, born of a woman' (Ga 4:4). At the close of the third session of the Second Vatican Council (21 November 1964), Paul VI proclaimed Mary 'Mother of the Church', a dignity originally promoted by

Polish bishops and favoured by John XXIII who had convoked the Council.

Our Lady of Lourdes

A tranquil town, in medieval times defended by a castle because of its strategic position between Tarbes and Pau in south-western France, Lourdes owes its present fame to Marie-Bernarde Soubirous (1844–79), whose pet name was Bernadette. Between 11 February and 16 July 1858, when she was fourteen, she experienced eighteen visions which, after exhaustive ecclesiastical investigations, were confirmed in January 1862 as apparitions of the Blessed Virgin Mary. To avoid unwelcome publicity, Bernadette retired to the convent of the Sisters of Charity and Christian Instruction at Nevers, enduring harsh discipline and much spiritual suffering. For her forbearance, simple faith and manifest integrity, she was beatified in 1925, canonized by Pius XI in 1933, and officially recorded as St Marie Bernarda (*f.d.*16 April). Her story, the *Song of Bernadette*, written in fulfilment of a vow made following his escape from occupied France by Franz Werfel, a German-Jewish writer, received world-wide acclaim.

Eldest daughter of indigent parents, brought up in conditions of near starvation, Bernadette survived the cholera epidemic of 1854 but remained sickly and asthmatic. She was granted her first vision when, gathering firewood near the river Gave de Pau, she was attracted by a noise, 'like the whispering wind', to a cleft in a rock known locally as Massabielle. There, as she later told her confessor in the local dialect, she saw *Aqueró*: 'this thing', a beautiful young lady who carried a rosary with a large, shining cross. Further details were provided after subsequent visions: the figure was that of a pretty young girl 'with a rosary over her arm'; like a little girl, dressed 'in a white robe with a blue girdle, a veil on her head, a yellow rose on each foot'; and resembling the statue of the Blessed Virgin in the parish church, but 'alive and surrounded by light'. When Lourdes became famous, Bernadette refused to acknowledge that the marble statue placed in the cave in 1862, prototype of figurines now sold to pilgrims, in any way resembled *Aqueró*.

From time to time the apparition addressed Bernadette politely in Bigourdan, the native patois, using not the intimate *tu* but the formal *vous*, and speaking some twelve sentences, including a call to penitence, a request that people should come in procession to the cave, and that a church should be built there. On the Feast of the Annunciation she identified herself in the local dialect as *Qué soy er' Immaculada Concepcioú*: 'I am the Immaculate

Conception'. This was four years after the definition of the dogma and almost three decades after the twenty-four-year-old Catherine Labouré, a novitiate of the Sisters of Charity of St Vincent de Paul, had been instructed by the Blessed Virgin to have struck in her honour the Miraculous Medal bearing the words, 'conceived without sin'. Bernadette agreed that the posture of the figure in the medal, insignia of the local Children of Mary, a pious sodality, resembled the lady whom she had seen in the cave.

The source of the curative waters at Lourdes was revealed on 25 February when a large crowd at the cave-mouth saw Bernadette recite a decade of her rosary and then, as she later related, obedient to the Lady's instructions, scratch the ground and drink a little water from a small muddy pool which welled up and within a week had become a torrent. Within a century of this event, five thousand cures by the water, carefully monitored by the Medical Bureau set up in 1882, had been reported, of which fifty-eight were declared miraculous.

After permission was granted in 1862 for the Blessed Virgin to be venerated at Lourdes, and in obedience to the command given to Bernadette, a church was built above the grotto and beside it in 1883–1900 the magnificent basilica of the Rosary. To mark the hundredth anniversary of Bernadette's visions, the future John XXIII, shortly before his election, dedicated there an underground auditorium capable of seating the thousands of worshippers who annually bring with them their chronically sick or seemingly incurable invalids. In impressive night processions they sing the Lourdes hymn, an English version of which, based on one by the Venerable Bede, was composed by Ronald A. Knox (1888–1957).

The Feast of Our Lady of Lourdes, an obligatory memorial on 11 February, the date of Bernadette's first vision, was declared universal in 1907. Shrines of Our Lady of Lourdes are numerous in the USA and Canada. Many paintings of Bernadette show the rose bush on which *Aquero* stood. If the flowers are in bloom, they recall the request that she should authenticate herself by making them blossom.

Visitation of the Blessed Virgin Mary

As proof that 'nothing is impossible to God', the angel Gabriel informed Mary that her kinswoman Elizabeth, barren wife of Zechariah, had conceived a son and was then in the sixth month of her pregnancy. Mary hastened to her cousin's home and remained with her until shortly before the birth of John the Baptist. Sixth-century pilgrims were shown the site of

Zechariah's summer residence, about six and a half kilometres from Jerusalem, near the village of Ain Karem: 'vineyard spring', where the Church of the Visitation now stands, near Mary's Well, on the terraced slopes of a mountain identified as the hill country of Judah where Mary met Elizabeth (Lk 1:39–56).

As Mary greeted Elizabeth, 'the child leapt in her womb', and this was interpreted as John's prenatal recognition of the presence of the Messiah. In the later Middle Ages the two babes were sometimes shown in the wombs of their respective mothers, John inclining his head as Jesus made a gesture of blessing, demonstrating that John, although like all mortals inheriting original sin, was thus sanctified before birth. This artistic convention, rare after the council of Trent, gave way to a more dignified rendering in which the prospective mothers embrace, Elizabeth, the elder figure, bowing or kneeling, as though saying, 'Who am I that the mother of my Lord should visit me?'

Filled with the Holy Spirit, Elizabeth uttered words later incorporated in the acclamation, *Ave Maria*: 'Hail Mary', 'Blessed are you among women and blessed is the fruit of your womb'. Mary responded with the *Magnificat*, the hymn sung at Vespers or Evensong, so called from the first word of the Latin text, *Magnificat anima mea Dominum*: 'My soul doth magnify the Lord'. Some early Latin manuscripts, which circulated before St Jerome produced the Vulgate translation of most of the Bible, attribute this canticle to Elizabeth, but more dependable Greek texts support the generally accepted attribution to Mary. Her song, one of rejoicing at the salvation of 'the poor in spirit, the faithful remnant of Israel', because God had put down the mighty from their thrones, filling the hungry with good things and sending the rich empty away, provided the theological inspiration for liberation movements in Latin America where poverty is endemic and devotion to Mary is widespread.

From the eighth century onwards the Visitation was the theme of lections in the Advent Embertide and during the week preceding Christmas, but there was no authorized commemoration of the event until Urban VI (1378–89) proposed a festival, hoping in vain that Mary's intercession would end the schism brought about by rival claims to the papacy. In 1401, Urban's successor, Boniface IX (1389–1404), declared the feast universal but it was observed only by those religious Orders which accepted his authority. The date chosen was 2 July, in the Eastern Church the festival commemorating the placing of the Holy Robe of the Mother of God in the church of Blachernae, a suburb of Constantinople.

In gratitude to Mary for the eventual ending of the schism, an attempt to re-establish the festival was made at the Council of Basle (1431–49), but it failed because the later acts of the Council were not universally recognized as having papal authority. Sixtus IV (1471–84), builder of the Sistine Chapel and a Franciscan devoted to the Virgin, following victories over the Turks by a fleet which he had financed, in 1475 finally instituted the festival, believing that it would secure Mary's continued assistance in his crusade. About 1482, after the recovery of Otranto, he dedicated to the Visitation the church of Santa Maria della Pace: 'Our Lady of Peace', restored in 1656 in baroque style by Pietro da Cortona.

As the feast was based on a scriptural passage, it was retained in the *Book of Common Prayer* as a Black Letter, or minor, festival, but was excluded from the *Alternative Service Book*. Logically, because it should fall before the Feast of the Nativity of John the Baptist on 24 June, it was moved in the Roman Catholic calendar of 1969 from 2 July to 31 May.

The Immaculate Heart of Mary

As well as promoting devotion to the Sacred Heart of Jesus (see p.82), St John Eudes initiated the analogous cult of the Holy Heart of Mary, symbol of her sinlessness, compassion and love for mankind. For a liturgical feast, first celebrated in 1648, he composed a Mass and Office, the texts of which were included in his somewhat diffuse work, *Le Coeur admirable de la très sainte Mère de Dieu* (1670): 'the wonderful heart of the most holy Mother of God'. Although the feast failed in 1669 to be approved by the Congregation of Rites, which supervised worship, it was permitted in certain localities. During the troubles of the Napoleonic era, in 1804 Pius VII (1800–23) allowed an analogous Mass of the Most Pure Heart of Mary.

Depiction of Mary's heart, pierced by a sword, on the obverse of the Miraculous Medal designed in accordance with supernatural instructions given to Catherine Labouré in 1830; definition of the dogma of the Immaculate Conception in 1854; approval in 1865 of a proper Mass based on that composed by St John Eudes; and the formation in 1877 of the Sons of the Immaculate Heart of Mary, its scapular, or badge, a pierced heart surrounded by flames, encircled with roses and surmounted by a lily: these developments culminated in repeated requests for official recognition of the devotion. These were reinforced in 1917 when the Virgin expressed the wish to the children to whom she appeared at Fátima, in Portugal, that the devotion should be established so that Russia would be saved, many souls converted, and that there would be peace. In recognition of his work, John Eudes, beatified in 1909, was canonized in 1925 (*f.d.*19 August).

On 31 October 1942, the twenty-fifth anniversary of the appearance at Fátima, Pius XII, seeking Mary's assistance during the terrible events of the Second World War, consecrated the whole world to the Immaculate Heart of Mary. Two years later, a feast of that name was instituted for 22 August, octave of the feast of the Immaculate Conception. In the revised Roman calendar of 1969, Saturday being the day traditionally devoted to Mary, it was moved to its present position, the second Saturday after the second Sunday after Pentecost, as an optional memorial, following the feast of the Sacred Heart of Jesus.

Our Lady of Mount Carmel

Overlooking the modern port of Haifa, Carmel, biblical synonym for beauty, a sacred promontory, 'the land blessed by God', was at an early period inhabited by Greek hermits who lived in beehive huts and caves and were devoted to the Blessed Virgin. After the establishment of the Kingdom of Jerusalem, the crusader Berthold of Limoges (*d.c.*1195), followed by St Brocard (*d.c.*1231; *f.d.*2 September), who was born in Jerusalem of Frankish parentage, assembled Latin solitaries into a monastic settlement on the headland and instituted the Brotherhood of the Blessed Virgin; they used the Latin liturgy, abstained from flesh-meat and dedicated themselves to poverty and prayer, observing a Rule granted to them in 1209 by Albert of Vercelli, Latin legate in Jerusalem.

The terrible slaughter which followed the Moslem conquest of Acre in 1291 forced surviving brothers to flee, and some of them eventually settled at Aylesford on the River Medway in Kent. There Simon (*c.*1165–1265), surnamed Stock because it was said he had lived in the hollow trunk ('stock') of a tree, had previously reorganized earlier refugees as mendicant, or 'begging', Carmelite friars. They wore a white mantle over a dark brown habit and were thus known as White Friars. For the same reason Carmelite Sisters, approved by Nicholas V on 7 October 1452, were called White Ladies.

When Henry VIII sequestrated the property of religious Orders, the friary at Aylesford became a private residence. It was re-established in 1942, some of Simon's relics being brought there in 1951, the rest remaining in the cathedral at Bordeaux, the city where he died. A statue in the chapel at Aylesford shows Simon receiving from the Virgin the brown Carmelite scapular, a strip of woollen material worn over a tunic. The tradition that, as a sign of grace, it would save whoever died wearing it from everlasting fire, appears late, in the so-called documents of Swaynton, which some consider to be a seventeenth-century forgery.

Carmelites have always promoted devotion to the Blessed Virgin Mary and actively defended the doctrine that she was free from taint of original sin. Their contemplative Order has fostered many renowned mystics, among them St Teresa of Avila (1515–82); her disciple, St John of the Cross (1542–91); and the Florentine, St Mary Magdalen of Pazzi (1566–1607). The autobiography, *Story of a Soul*, and the healing miracles attributed to her intercession, caused the Carmelite convent where St Thérèse (1873–97) lived at Lisieux to become a great centre for pilgrimages, especially after her canonization in 1925.

The convent on Mount Carmel, refounded in 1769, was destroyed in 1799 when Turks slaughtered Napoleon's wounded and sick soldiers sheltering there, and rebuilt in 1827; enthroned over the altar is the statue of Our Lady of Mount Carmel, carved in 1836 by Caraventa, a Genoese sculptor. The original patronal feast of the Order was 15 August, but 16 May, the date of the approbation of the Rule in 1226 by Honorius III, was kept in England as Simon's feast day, and approved for the Carmelite Order in 1564, although he was never formally canonized. A festival commemorating Simon's vision, believed to have happened on 16 July, was permitted in 1564 and made universal by Benedict XIII (1724–30). It was retained in 1969 as an optional memorial.

Dedication of Santa Maria Maggiore

The church of Santa Maria Maggiore, called 'major' because it is one of the four great Roman basilicas and the mother-church of all those which bear the Blessed Virgin's name, was dedicated to her by St Sixtus (or Xystus) III (432–40) in thanksgiving for the agreement reached in 433 between St Cyril of Alexandria and the bishops of Antioch over the two natures of Christ, human and divine, united in one person. Mosaics within the church depicting Mary enthroned, adorned with jewels like a Byzantine empress and attended by angels, also demonstrated Sixtus' orthodoxy in that he supported the decision of the Council of Ephesus (431) to confer on her the title, 'Mother of God'.

Archaeological research has shown that the name 'Liberian basilica', given to Santa Maria Maggiore, is a misnomer, originating in two entries in the *Liber Pontificalis* relating to Liberius (352–66): 'Here he built a basilica in his name near the market of Livia'; and 'He [Sixtus] built near Livia's market [on the Esquiline hill] the basilica which formerly bore the name of Liberius'. In fact Sixtus' foundation was some distance away from Liberius' church although, as was common practice, it incorporated material taken from the earlier building.

This misunderstanding over the role of Liberius was perpetuated in a fourteenth-century legend which explained why the dedication festival on 5 August, made universal in 1568 by St Pius V (now an optional memorial), was named *ad Nives*: 'of the snow'. Depicted on a mosaic, now obscured, on the façade of the church and in two large lunettes which Bartolomé Esteban Murillo painted between 1662 and 1665 for the reconstructed baroque church of Santa María la Blanca in Seville, it relates the appearance of St Mary to Giovanni Patrizio: 'John the Patrician', and his wife, a childless couple who had willed all their possessions to her. They were told to build a church in her honour on the Esquiline hill where, although it was August, the height of the Roman summer, they would find the outline of the basilica on the snow-covered ground, as indeed they did when they went there with Liberius, to whom they had related their dream. (Alternative versions are that Liberius drew the plan with his pastoral staff and that the church was built where the Virgin had left her footprints.)

In 1742 a commission recommended that the title, *Santa Maria della Neve*: 'Our Lady of the Snow', should no longer be used, but it survived in baptismal names and in the dedication of churches in high, snow-covered mountain regions. A shower of white rose-petals descended like snowflakes when the commemorative Mass was celebrated in the Borghese chapel of the basilica.

Another title, *Santa Maria ad Praesepe*: 'St Mary of the Crib', associates the basilica with pieces of wood from the manger in Bethlehem, or from the cradle (*culla*) in which the infant Jesus was carried on the flight into Egypt. These relics are kept beneath the altar in the Sistine Chapel, built in 1589 by Sixtus V. The six-foot-high silver and crystal reliquary which contains them, donated by the Duchess of Villahermosa, replaced the one given by Margaret of Austria, wife of Philip III of Spain, which was looted by French soldiers during the Napoleonic invasion of Italy. After the pope has said the dawn Mass on Christmas Day, the relics are exposed until Vespers.

The Assumption of the Blessed Virgin Mary

There are conflicting traditions as to what happened to Mary after the last mention of her as engaged in constant prayer in the company of Jesus' brethren (or close relations), the apostles and several of his women followers (Ac I:12–14). One view was that, in her grief, she did not long survive the death of her son: another that she settled in Ephesus with John, traditionally the 'beloved disciple' to whom Jesus had entrusted her.

A church dedicated to Mary, built on the site of what may have been the stock exchange of the ancient city, was the meeting-place of the Council of Ephesus (431) which declared her 'Mother of God'. In 1914, a ruined dwelling at Panaghia Kapouli, on Mount Solemissos, south of Ephesus, which fitted the description of the house in which Mary lived with John as seen in a vision granted to Anna Katharina Emmerick (1774–1824), an Augustinian nun, was declared a sacred site. It was also said that Mary returned to Jerusalem, or indeed had continued to live there, until she ended her days where the modern abbey of the Dormition, built on the site of Mary's 'falling asleep', now stands.

These traditions posed a dilemma, because it was inconceivable that Mary's sinless body, likened to the Ark of the Covenant which was made of incorruptible wood, should suffer putrefaction. The text, 'Rise thou and the ark of thy strength' (Ps 132/1:8) was understood to mean that it was God's will that, as Christ had ascended, so too Mary would in due course be received into heaven. Non-canonical writings, circulating in many languages, explained how this came about. Reduced to essentials, they related that Mary, warned of her approaching end by an angel, usually St Michael who conducts souls to heaven, was surrounded on her death-bed by the apostles, miraculously transported from their various mission-fields. Jesus appeared, bore away her soul, and returned three days after her burial, when angels carried her body to Paradise where it was reunited with her soul under the Tree of Life.

Although one of the legends condemned as tainted with heresy in a decree attributed to St Gelasius (492–96), it nevertheless gained wide currency in the West, being accepted by St Gregory of Tours (c.538–94) and depicted in carvings on church portals, in breviaries and in paintings of the death of the Virgin. After the Council of Trent, it was replaced as a theme in art by the depiction of Mary's bodily ascension, but borne up to heaven by angels, in contrast to the ascension of Christ, who rises up by his own power.

At an early period Mary was honoured in Jerusalem on 15 August, possibly the date of the dedication of a church named after her. To avoid confusion with other Marian feasts, the Byzantine Emperor Maurice in 600 declared this the festival of Mary's Dormition, or 'falling asleep', also known as her 'Passing over' (*Transitus*). It was adopted in Rome in the time of Theodore I (642–49), a pope of Greek parentage, and seemingly a refugee from the Arab invasion of Jerusalem. St Aldhelm (639–709), abbot of Malmesbury and bishop of Sherborne, noted that in England Mary's 'anniversary' (*natalis*, the commemoration of the death of a saint) was kept 'in the middle of August'. In medieval times it was known as 'Mary-Mass', or 'Our Lady in Harvest', but was suppressed, along with other holidays, in 1549, because it took labourers away from their work. In contrast, in Catholic countries it continued to be one of the most popular festivals of the year, its theological justification, accepted without question, declared by Benedict XIV (1740–58) to be an opinion which it would be blasphemous to contradict. The increased number and magnificence of paintings of Mary's ascension from the late sixteenth century onwards, in which Mary appears as 'a woman, adorned with the sun, standing on the moon, and with twelve stars on her head for a crown', attests the depth of popular devotion to this manifestation of divine grace bestowed on the Mother of God (Rv 12:1).

On 1 November 1950, in response to popular demand, and fortified by the almost universal and positive response by his bishops to his question, whether this pious belief should be dogmatically defined as a binding statement of faith, Pius XII issued the Apostolic Constitution, *Munificentissimus Deus*, in which it was affirmed that Mary, 'when the course of her earthly life was finished . . . was assumed [Latin *assumpta est*: 'taken up'] body and soul into the glory of heaven'. Pronouncements on the vexed questions as to whether Mary did or did not die, and as to the manner of her ascension to heaven were avoided by the use in the document of phrases such as, 'death having been conquered' and 'preserved from the corruption of the tomb'. Paul VI, in his *Solemn Profession of Faith* (30 June 1968), expressed the present understanding of those who accept the fact of Mary's reception into heaven when he stated, 'She received in anticipation the future lot of all the just'. This sentiment is echoed in the opening prayer of the Mass for the Assumption of the Blessed Virgin Mary, a solemnity on 15 August, which ends, 'May we see heaven as our final goal and come to share her glory'.

In the *American Prayer Book* and in the revised Prayer Books of some other Anglican provinces, but not in the *Alternative Service Book*, the day is entered in the calendar as 'Saint Mary the Virgin, Mother of Our Lord Jesus

Christ', without dogmatic commitment, although the prayer, 'Grant that we, who have been redeemed by his blood, may share with her the glory of thine eternal kingdom', lends itself to an assumptionist interpretation.

Queenship of Mary

In the Latin liturgy the title 'Queen of Heaven', long familiar in the works of Eastern writers, was applied to Mary at least as early as the thirteenth century. She was so addressed in anthems in the Divine Office: *Ave, Regina Caelorum*: 'Hail, Queen of Heavens', of unknown authorship but attributed to St Bernard of Clairvaux (1090–1153); and *Regina caeli, laetare!*: 'Queen of Heaven, rejoice!', said or sung standing from Easter to Pentecost. The antiphon, *Salve Regina*: 'Hail Queen', probably composed by the Blessed Herman the Cripple (1013–54) and popularized by the Cistercian Order, was sung by the souls in Dante's *Paradiso* and, according to Christopher Columbus' *Journal*, was taught by his sailors to the inhabitants of Guanahuaní, the first island that they sighted in the Caribbean. Mary crowned, or being crowned on her reception into heaven, was a popular representation of her in art.

When Pius XII on 1 November 1950 solemnly defined the dogma of the Assumption of Mary, he stated that she was raised body and soul to the glory of heaven, 'to shine resplendent as Queen at the right hand of her Son'. On 11 October 1954, during the Marian year which marked the centenary of the proclamation of the dogma of the Immaculate Conception, he established the feast of the Queenship of Mary on 31 May, intended 'to renew the ancient devotion to Mary as Queen, whose royal dignity rests on her divine motherhood'. After the Second Vatican Council the feast, an obligatory memorial, was transferred to 22 August so that it now follows appropriately the feast of the Assumption on 15 August.

Birthday of the Blessed Virgin Mary

A Latin work, *The Nativity of Mary*, improbably attributed to St Jerome, stated that Mary was born in the very house in which the angel Gabriel appeared to her. An unknown pilgrim from Piacenza, Italy, was shown *c*.570 at Sepphoris (now Saffuriya, or Zippori), some six kilometres north of Nazareth, the chair in which she was sitting. A rival version located Joachim and Anna (the names given to Mary's parents in the non-canonical *Book of James*) in Jerusalem where, near St Stephen's Gate, known in Arabic as *Bab*

Sitti Maryam: 'Gate of the Lady Mary', a third-century oratory, discovered beneath the crusader church of St Anne (restored 1863–77), is said to have been built on the site of their home. It was explained that they fled there after Roman troops pillaged Sepphoris, then the capital of Galilee.

Unless it was the date of the dedication of a church, possibly endowed by the Empress Eudocia near the basilica of St Stephen (consecrated 1 June 460), the saint to whom she was devoted, it is not known why 8 September was chosen for the festival of the Nativity of Mary. Although of local observance in the West and included in the calendars of some religious Orders, it fell into abeyance but was revived in the thirteenth century. One medieval legend attributed its institution to the report given to the pope of angelic voices heard on the eve of 8 September celebrating the birth of Mary: another relates that the feast was ordered by Innocent IV (1243–54) in fulfilment of a vow made at the time, following the death of Celestine IV in 1241, when the cardinals were shut up in deliberately unbearable conditions until they could agree on a successor.

In 1549 Cranmer omitted the Festival of the Nativity from the *Prayer Book*, although it was in the Sarum calendar. It was reinstated as a Black Letter day, a lesser festival, in the *Book of Common Prayer*, but was left out of the revised *American Prayer Book*; in compensation, 15 August was given Red Letter status as a major festival. In contrast, to avoid associating that date with the dogma of the Assumption, but wishing to honour Mary, it was decided to omit it from the calendar of the *Alternative Service Book* but to include 8 September as one of the Greater Holy Days, with the neutral title 'The Blessed Virgin Mary'.

Our Lady of Sorrow

Simeon's words to Mary when she came to the Temple, 'and a sword will pierce your soul, too' (Lk 2:35), were understood by most Latin Fathers of the Church to refer to the sorrows which she would experience during her son's lifetime. By the fifteenth century, contrasting with Mary's joys, these totalled the symbolic number seven, the fifth inspiring the famous sequence, *Stabat Mater Dolorosa*: 'the sorrowful mother stood at the foot of the cross', probably composed by the Blessed Jacopone da Todi (*c*.1230–1306), a Franciscan.

The feast, now an obligatory memorial, originated in a devotion practised by the Order of the Servants of the Blessed Virgin Mary, known as Servites, founded in 1233 when seven wealthy city councillors of Florence renounced the world and resolved to devote themselves to her service. In 1668 they were given permission to celebrate the feast of the Seven Sorrows, made universal by Pius VII in 1814 in thanksgiving to the Virgin for his release from captivity in Fontainebleau and his return to Rome. Pius X reassigned it in 1913 to 15 September, the date on which it is now celebrated. To avoid a festival in Lent, and the anomaly of two feasts with a similar content, the 'Commemoration of the distress and sorrow of the Blessed Virgin', celebrated in Cologne in 1423 and extended to the whole Latin Church by Benedict XIII in 1727, was omitted from the calendar in 1969.

Our Lady of the Rosary

In his Apostolic Exhortation *Marialis Cultus* (1974), Paul VI approved the saying of the rosary before Mass, that is praying and meditating on episodes in the life of Jesus Christ and his mother, classified as joyful, sorrowful and glorious. Count is kept of these prayers by the use of a mnemonic device, a string of beads known as a rosary (Latin *rosarium*: 'rose garden'), peculiar to Mary because she is the rose of Sharon of the *Song of Songs* (Sg 2:1).

According to William of Malmesbury (c.1090–1143), the famous Lady Godiva, wife of Leofric, earl of Mercia, when she died c.1041 left to the Benedictine monastery which she had founded 'a circlet of gems that she had threaded on a string, so that touching them one by one as she repeated her prayers, she might not fall short of the exact number'. A legend, stoutly defended, and equally hotly contested, nevertheless attributed the origin of the modern rosary to the appearance of the Blessed Virgin to St Dominic (1170–1221), founder of the Order of Preachers, known as Dominicans, when she presented him with a rosary, saying that to combat the Albigensians, who denied the divinity of Christ, he should persuade them to use it for the constant repetition of 'Hail, Mary', the angelic salutation.

This devotion, in which meditations on the mysteries of the life of Christ were interspersed with 'Hail, Mary', was undoubtedly fostered by Dominicans who encouraged its use in Confraternities of the Virgin, founded after the liberation of Cologne in 1474 from Burgundian invaders, was seen as the result of the continuous repetition of the rosary during the siege. St Pius V (1556–72), a Dominican, declared that an annual feast of Our Lady of Victory should be kept in recognition of Mary's intercession which secured victory over the Turkish fleet at Lepanto on that day in 1571. His successor, Gregory XIII, in 1573, fixed the festival on the first Sunday in October and renamed it Our Lady of the Rosary. In thanksgiving for another victory over the Turks, won by Prince Eugène of Savoie-Carigan at Peterwardein (Petrovard, Yugoslavia) on 5 August, feast of the dedication of Santa Maria Maggiore, Clement XI made the festival universal. It is now an obligatory memorial, observed on 7 October, the date of the victory at Lepanto.

The Presentation of the Blessed Virgin in the Temple

That Mary was divinely appointed to bear the Saviour, and preserved pure for his virginal conception, is an ancient and fundamental belief. How this came about was explained in the tradition incorporated in the non-canonical *Book of James*, probably compiled in the mid-second century. The scriptural model was the story of Samuel, the last judge of Israel, whose barren mother, Hannah, vowed that if she were given a son she would dedicate him to the Lord God. When the child was born she called him Samuel, 'because the Lord had heard her', and when he was weaned, in fulfilment of her vow, presented him at the shrine at Shiloh where he was brought up by the priests (I S I:1–28).

In like manner, Joachim and Anna, miraculously granted Mary, made a sanctuary for her in her bedchamber where she was cared for by virgin daughters of Jerusalem. When she was three years old she was escorted to the Temple where she was received by Zechariah, the High Priest, future father of John the Baptist. She remained there, fed by an angel, until she reached the age of puberty. Joseph was then chosen by a miracle to be her husband. Mary, the Ark of the New Covenant, had thus come to the Temple in the same way as Moses was commanded to place the Ark of the Testimony in the Tent of Meeting (Ex 40:21). This legend was depicted by Giotto di Bondone (*c.*1267–1337) in the fresco cycle which covers the interior of the Arena Chapel at Padua.

The date chosen for the festival in the Orthodox Church was 20 November, when in 543 a basilica in honour of Mary was consecrated, identified as standing near the Temple, in front of the mosque of Al Aqsa. Although included in the calendars of monasteries of the Order of St Benedict and in the Canterbury *Benedictional*, the book containing the words of the bishop's blessings, there was no formal recognition of the feast in the West until 1371 when Philip de Mésières, a French knight, on his return from Cyprus, and with the support of Charles V of France, persuaded Gregory XI to permit Franciscans to celebrate on that day the

Office and Mass which he had composed. Although adopted in many places, and included in the Breviary by Sixtus IV (1471–84), a Franciscan devoted to Mary, it was removed by St Pius V (1566–72) and the feast did not achieve full recognition until Sixtus V (1585–90) made it universal. It is now an obligatory memorial, celebrated on 21 November, its significance being the fact that from her earliest moments Mary was dedicated to Christ.

The Immaculate Conception of the Blessed Virgin Mary

A *typicon*, a liturgical manual of the Orthodox Church, attributed to St Sabas (439–542) but with later additions, reveals that in the seventh century there was a feast called Conception of St Anne, so named in accordance with the Eastern custom of associating conception with the person who conceives, not the one conceived. The date was 9 December, approximately nine months before the feast of the birth of Mary on 8 September in the following year. The festival was observed in regions in the West where Greek influence prevailed and was known in Normandy, possibly introduced there after the Norman invasion of Sicily.

The feast was instituted, or reinstituted, in England by Elsinus, or Aethelsiga, abbot of Ramsey in Huntingdonshire (who figures as Helsyn, or Elpyn, in a medieval collection of miracles of the Virgin), apparently in fulfilment of a vow made when he survived a storm at sea on his return from exile on the continent (1087/8). Contacts between Canterbury and Lyons may have inspired the canons of the cathedral in that city to celebrate the feast *c*.1139–40. This provoked an indignant letter from St Bernard, abbot of the Cistercian house at Clairvaux, censuring the canons for introducing 'a new festival of which the Church knows nothing and which reason does not approve, nor ancient tradition hand down to us'. It was proper that Mary's birth should be celebrated, but mindful of the text 'in sin did my mother conceive me' (Ps 51/50:5), he could not approve it if it were implied that there was holiness in Mary's conception. This would imply that she was conceived by the Holy Spirit and not by man, 'which would be a thing unheard of'.

In this way St Bernard stated the case against the opposing view that Mary, chosen before time to bear Christ, was the unique exception and that the moment of her conception was 'immaculate' (Latin *immaculata*: 'spotless'), free from original sin, the state of estrangement from God, 'original' because it was the inheritance of the disobedience of Adam and

Eve. St Anselm (*c.*1033–1109), archbishop of Canterbury, humbly admitted that 'in the secrets of so great a matter there is something of which we are ignorant', but Eadmer, his pupil and biographer, explained in a syllogism later glossed by John Duns Scotus (*c.*1264–1308), the Oxford philosopher, 'God could do it; it was fitting that he should do it; therefore he did it'.

The debate lasted for centuries, the point at issue being: at what moment in her mother's womb was Mary, conceived in the natural way, freed from the inheritance of sin, whether, according to the Franciscans, by a special act of God at her conception, or, as proposed by the Dominicans, when the rational soul was infused in the foetus, supposedly eighty days after conception in the case of a female. (Although gynaecological knowledge has advanced since those days, the question 'When is a foetus a person?' is still relevant to the present debate over contraception and abortion.) Paul V (1605–21), who favoured the Franciscan view, forbade anything to be said in public contrary to Mary's sinlessness and Gregory XV (1621–3) extended the ban to private discussions.

Pressure for the dogmatic resolution of the question increased in the early nineteenth century as devotion to Mary, an answer to the secularism of the age, intensified. Gregory XVI (1831–46) promoted the Immaculate Conception of the Blessed Virgin but did not go so far as defining it as a matter of faith. Pius IX (1846–78), who ascribed to Mary his cure from epilepsy which otherwise would have prevented his becoming a priest, settled the matter when he promulgated the Apostolic Constitution *Ineffabilis Deus* (8 December 1854) in which, following Duns Scotus, he declared that 'in the first instant of her conception', Mary 'by a singular grace and privilege, was preserved free from all stain of original sin'.

Theological subtleties did not trouble the populace. St Anne resting in bed as midwives bathe the newborn Mary was a frequent genre scene from the fourteenth century onwards. When he was a soldier, St Ignatius of Loyola (*c.*1491–1556) threatened with a dagger a man who denied Mary's sinlessness. Sixtus IV (1471–84), a Franciscan, approved in 1476 the feast of the Immaculate Conception with its own Mass and Office. It was made universal in 1708. Meanwhile the pictorial representation of Mary, identified by St Bonaventure as the 'Woman clothed with the Sun . . . a crown of twelve stars above her head' (Rv 12:1), became a powerful propaganda reply to Protestant criticism of Marian devotion. As she was in the divine mind before time, on the evidence of the text 'God created me, first fruits of his fashioning' (Pr 8:22), Mary was cast as a young virgin, looking downwards as she descended towards the globe of the earth, or standing on a crescent

Moon, the symbol of birth. A serpent beneath her feet, illustrating the text 'She will bruise your head' (Gn 3:15.Vg), indicated that she was the New Eve, reversing the original sin of Eden and freed from it at the moment of her conception.

A solemnity on 8 December in the Roman calendar, the festival is not celebrated by Protestants, unable to accept the doctrine of the Immaculate Conception, but in the Anglo-Catholic tradition it is listed either as 'Conception of the Blessed Virgin', or, more adventurously, it is given the prefix 'Immaculate'. This is the last Marian feast of the year, the conclusion of the round of celebrations in her honour, the liturgical recognition of her God-given status in relation to her divine Son and her dignity as archetype of the Church.

Commemoration of the Saints

WHEN PAUL GREETED MEMBERS OF THE NEWLY-established Christian communities at Ephesus, Corinth and Rome as 'saints', he implied, using a Hebrew concept, that they were consecrated to the deity, 'called to be his holy people' (Rm 1:7). In this sense all baptized Christians are saints, sanctified through Jesus, 'the Holy One of God' (Jn 6:69). Before the end of the century, however, the attribute 'holy' (Latin *sanctus*) had acquired a special significance, when, falsely accused of crimes against the state, of dishonouring the gods and of hatred of the human race, many Christians suffered persecution and death.

Tacitus, the Roman historian, described in his *Annals* how the Emperor Nero in July 64 fixed on Christians the blame for the Great Fire of Rome and had their bodies nailed to crosses and set alight so that they illuminated his pleasure-gardens. When the Fifth Seal was broken, the writer of *The Revelation to John* saw beneath the altar 'the souls of all the people who had been killed on account of the Word of God'. These were the saints who were admonished to be patient until, their white robes 'washed in the blood of the Lamb', they would stand in front of God's throne, their reward for accepting death rather than denying their faith (Rv 6:9–11; 7:13–17; 14:12).

Saints without number suffered during intermittent but terrifying persecutions which lasted almost until 313 when the Emperor Constantine declared Christianity to be a tolerated religion. They were accounted 'martyrs' (Greek *martus*: 'witness examined in a law court') who steadfastly maintained their testimony to Christ even in the face of death. One of the many whose *Acts* were recorded was Polycarp, bishop of Smyrna, who c.155 chose to be stabbed and immolated by fire rather than curse his Lord, saying, 'Eighty-six years have I served him, and he has done me no wrong: how then can I blaspheme my King who saved me?' His fellow-Christians gathered up his bones, 'more valuable than precious stones', and each year commemorated the anniversary of his martyrdom, an early example of the cult of saints and of the veneration of their relics.

In more peaceful times violent death was no longer accounted a necessary qualification for the title 'martyr'. Ascetics, teachers, bishops and other defenders of the faith, through self-denial and perseverance in following Christ, had also borne witness to him. These were the 'confessors' who had 'confessed', or avowed, their religion in face of all worldly distractions. They too were numbered among the saints and entered in the martyrologies, the records, kept at first by each local community, of the dates of their deaths, or rather of their rebirth into the glory of heaven, and of the shrines in cemeteries outside cities where each year they were remembered.

As their fame spread and their relics were diffused, an official list, or 'canon', became necessary, particularly because the Church was perceived as one body, one family, united in Christ in heaven and on earth. Through the Son, saints had been granted communion with the Father but they in turn were joined in communion with Christians on earth. They could therefore be invoked, called upon either in the Mass or in private intercessions to pray on behalf of the faithful. Local bishops initially controlled the canonization, or entry in the approved list, of those whom the public deemed to be saints, but from 933, when John XV, at a synod in the Lateran, the cathedral of Rome, agreed to a request for the solemn canonization of Ulrich (923–73), bishop of Augsburg, the pope claimed the prerogative. An example of the exercise of this right was Alexander III's consent in 1161 to the canonization of Edward the Confessor (1003–66) who founded Westminster Abbey, where his tomb may still be seen.

At the time of the Reformation, Hugh Latimer, bishop of Worcester, who was burnt at Oxford on 16 October 1555 in the reign of Queen Mary, rejected canonization as 'judging of men before the Lord's judgment'. The Reformers also objected to the invocation of saints, and the more extreme among them, reacting against medieval abuses, sought the complete abolition of saints' days because they obscured Sunday observance and the preaching of the word of God.

Less radical was the position in 1536 of the members of Convocation who, although declaring that the number of holy days was 'the occasion of much sloth and idleness', asked only that some should be abolished. Saints' days nevertheless had played such a prominent part in the lives of the people, permitting respite from labour, dating, and the beginning of university and law terms, that in 1561 Queen Elizabeth directed the Royal Commissioners for Ecclesiastical Causes to draw up a new list which would meet both liturgical and civil requirements. With certain omissions and additions this list formed the basis of the holy days authorized in the *Book of Common Prayer* and, although revised, also of those permitted in other Prayer Books of the Anglican Communion. The principles governing selection, although with anomalies, were to include only those persons mentioned in the Bible; certain ancient saints; and many British saints. A distinction was made between Red Letter days, those marked in red, for which collect, epistle and gospel were provided, and Black Letter days, feasts printed in black.

The Reformation break with Rome and the consequent rejection of the Holy See's right to canonize meant that in England there was no ecclesiastical process whereby the list could be extended to include those who by their lives and example were judged worthy to be numbered among the saints. Commissions in the USA and England therefore investigated at the time of liturgical revision in the twentieth century the claims of many who should be remembered. The *American Prayer Book* now lists, among others, Phillips Brooks, bishop of Massachusetts, known for his Christmas hymn, 'O Little Town of Bethlehem'; Absalom Jones, the first black person ordained in the American Episcopal Church; and John and Charles Wesley who, although called 'Methodists', remained within the Church of England. The *Alternative Service Book* includes Charles I, king and martyr, and Josephine Butler (1828–1906), social reformer, who fought for the suppression of 'white slavery' and the reclamation of prostitutes. Both Churches commemorate the medieval mystic Julian of Norwich, revered by feminists; the poet George Herbert; and Charles Simeon (1759–1836), leader of the Evangelical revival, balanced (a characteristic Anglican compromise) by Edward King (1829–1910), bishop of Lincoln, who survived prosecution for 'ritualism', the introduction of ceremonial practices in Anglican services.

The process of canonization in the Roman Catholic Church, now in the hands of the Congregation for the Causes of Saints, was formalized in the seventeenth century when a promoter, popularly known as 'the devil's advocate', was required to make a critical examination of the life and alleged miracles of the person proposed for sainthood. The result could be beatification, which permits the title of 'Blessed' and public veneration in certain churches, dioceses and religious Orders; or inscription in the catalogue of saints which, among other honours, allows a festival day, a Mass and Office, and invocation in public prayers.

In ancient Rome the register of accounts due for settlement on the *kalendae*: 'first days of the month', was called a *kalendarium*: 'calendar', a word which found its way into ecclesiastical usage to designate the table of holy days and saints' days to be celebrated during the year. Almost 1,500 saints could claim inclusion in the Roman calendar when Alban Butler, a Catholic from Appletree in Northamptonshire educated at the English College at Douai in northern France, published his monumental *The Lives of the Fathers, Martyrs and Principal Saints* (1756–59). In the 1966 revision of his work there were approximately a thousand more entries. This illustrates the complexity of the task facing the compilers of the General Roman Calendar of 1969, despite earlier revisions of the *Breviary* which had reduced the number.

The solution to the problem of selection was to exclude many saints of doubtful historicity – for example, Barbara who was shut up in a tower – although because of her popularity they retained Cecilia, patroness of musicians; nor could George, patron saint of England, be left out. Instead they concentrated on saints of universal fame while permitting the veneration of others who had special links with particular countries, churches and religious Orders. They also included some recent saints like Charles Lwanga and Companions who were put to death in Uganda in 1885 and canonized in 1964. Nevertheless, however selective the intent, most days of the year were filled with a considerable number of commemorations. The principal festivals were therefore ranked in order of importance as solemnities, feasts, memorials and optional memorials, others being left to the discretion of local councils of bishops where their celebration was customary.

Within the compass of the present work it is obviously impossible to discuss even a small number of important saints. Instead notes are added below on a few representative festivals.

John the Baptist

The forerunner who announced the coming of Christ had three festivals to his name. His conception was commemorated on 24 September, the date when it was assumed that the angel appeared to Zechariah, his father (Lk I:8–25), confirmed by the fact that Elizabeth, his mother, was six months pregnant on 25 March when Gabriel was sent to Mary (Lk I:36). His birth (a solemnity) is accordingly celebrated on 24 June, three months later and six months before the nativity of Jesus on 25 December, the difference of a day being attributable to methods of dating in the Julian calendar. As the June date coincided with the summer solstice when the days begin to shorten, St Augustine of Hippo saw it as the fulfilment of John's statement regarding Jesus, 'He must increase as I decrease'. The beheading (or 'decollation') of John because he denounced as adulterous Herod's marriage to Herodias, his half-brother's former wife (Mt 14:1–12), attested in Josephus' *Antiquities of the Jews* (XVIII:V:12), although thought to have taken place around Passover, is commemorated on 29 August (a memorial), the date when his supposed head was discovered. It is preserved in the Church of St Silvester *in capite* in Rome.

The Holy Innocents

The children of Bethlehem, 'from two years old and under', who were slain on the orders of Herod in his search for the infant Jesus (Mt 2:16) are accounted martyrs because they shed their blood for Christ. Although there could not have been more than a score of them in this small village, early commentators equated them with the 144,000 who had 'kept their virginity and not been defiled with women' (Rv 14:4), hence they were 'innocents'. Their feast on 28 December was known in England as Childermas.

Joseph, husband of Mary

Although Joseph was mentioned in some ninth-century martyrologies and commemorated at Winchester and some other English cathedrals after the Norman Conquest, he was mostly neglected in the Middle Ages. A figure of fun in medieval drama and depicted in art as an old man, pondering on the mystery of the virginal conception of Jesus, he was thought, on the evidence of the *Book of James*, to be about eighty-six years of age and therefore incapable of being the child's progenitor.

Jean Gerson (1363–1429), a French mystical writer, initiated the reaction to this travesty and urged the need for a feast in honour of Joseph; it was eventually approved in 1480 by Sixtus IV and made universal by Gregory XV, and is now a solemnity on 19 March. St Bernardino of Siena (1380–1444), the eloquent Franciscan preacher, promoted Joseph as the ideal earthly father, a change in status which is thereafter observable in art, Joseph becoming a vigorous, youngish man, fully capable of fostering the child. In the Gospels his occupation (in Greek) is given as 'craftsman', but he is traditionally described as a carpenter and shown with the tools of his trade. This impelled Pius XII in 1955 to establish an additional festival on 1 May (now an optional memorial) of 'St Joseph, Workman, patron of artisans'.

The Chair of Peter the Apostle

In the central apse of St Peter's basilica in Rome, encased in the gilded bronze throne, a setting designed by Gianlorenzo Bernini (1598–1680), is a portable wooden chair (*cathedra*), dating from the ninth century but said to be the chair on which Peter sat as first bishop of Rome. 'The festival of St Peter of the Chair' (now a feast) on 22 February is recorded in the so-called *Chronograph of 354*, a date which may have been that of a dedication of a church containing a statue of him, seated like a classical teacher, but which curiously coincides with the day on which Roman families held a banquet in honour of their ancestors, a practice which was continued by Christians and, as late as the sixth century, censured in a decree of the Council of Tours (567).

Peter and Paul

It is an ancient tradition that these two apostles, who are frequently depicted together in early Christian art, were martyred on the same day in the same year, when Nero was emperor. Peter was crucified head-downwards, according to Origen, because he held himself unworthy to be put on the cross in the same way as his Lord, and Paul was beheaded because, unlike Peter, he was a Roman citizen. The *Chronograph of 354* has an entry for 29 June (now a solemnity): 'Peter at the catacombs [some read 'at the Vatican'] and Paul on the Ostian Way in the Consulate of Tuscus and Bassus' (i.e. 258), which may refer to the places of burial of their relics. The liturgical festival on this day, assumed to be that of their martyrdom, may have begun when these relics, removed for safety in 258 to the catacombs of St Sebastian, were returned to churches built on the earlier sites during the reign of the Emperor Constantine.

Mary Magdalene

Mary, who came from the village of Magdal, north of Tiberias, near the Lake of Galilee, was the woman 'out of whom came seven devils', which may mean that Jesus cured her of epilepsy which was then attributed to demonic possession (Lk 8:2). She witnessed the crucifixion; saw where Jesus' body was laid; and was the first person to whom the risen Christ appeared (Mk 16:9).

In art Mary's attribute is a jar of ointment because it was an ancient opinion, supported by St Gregory the Great (590–604), that she, Mary of Bethany and the unnamed woman who approached Jesus in the house of the Pharisee (or of Simon the Leper) and anointed him as he sat at table were one and the same person. It was generally assumed, although without positive support in the Greek text, that the latter, described as 'a woman of the city who was a sinner', which could mean that she had transgressed the rabbinic code, was a prostitute (Lk 7:37). For this reason it was the custom in some places on her festival (22 July, since the thirteenth century, now a memorial) to preach to women of the streets on the theme of forgiveness, echoing Jesus' words, 'Your faith has saved you; go in peace'. A ninth-century legend that Mary spent the last years of her life in penitence in a cave at Sainte-Baume, near Marseilles, and was then received into heaven was cited as an example for all who had fallen.

Since 1969, in accordance with the view of St Ambrose of Milan, and as is the practice of the Orthodox Churches, Mary Magdalene is distinguished in the calendar from the other personages with whom she was formerly equated.

Apostles and Evangelists

Jesus chose twelve of his disciples to be his apostles (Greek *apostolos*: 'emissary') who would spread the gospel first to 'the lost sheep of Israel' and then to all mankind. Their names, listed in varying order, in certain cases pose problems of identity. Matthias was chosen by lot to replace Judas Iscariot (Ac 1:26). James, 'the Lord's brother (or cousin)', although not originally one of the twelve, was also accounted an apostle because the risen Christ had appeared to him (I Cor 15:7). This title was later extended to Paul after his conversion on the road to Damascus and to Barnabas, 'a good man, full of the Holy Spirit', traditionally the first bishop of Cyprus.

One of the four canonical Gospels is ascribed to Matthew (also called Levi) and another to John, son of Zebedee, thought to be 'the disciple Jesus loved'. These disciples are therefore styled 'apostles and evangelists', whereas Luke, Paul's 'fellow-worker', and Mark, described by Papias in the second century as 'Peter's interpreter', are 'evangelists'.

Information about the activities of some of these personalities may be gleaned in many cases from the scriptures: others are but names. Non-canonical sources, mostly legendary, although possibly preserving older traditions, have supplied further information about them. The dates assigned for their festivals depended upon the time of the discovery of their relics; the translation of remains; and the dedication of churches in their honour.

Andrew (30 November) was one of the earliest of the apostles to enter the calendar. This happened after his relics were brought from Patras, where it was said he was martyred, to Constantinople, in the reign of Constantius II (337–40). His status as patron saint of Scotland was derived from the legend that, as the result of a vision, some of his bones were carried by St Regulus (or Rule) to Kilrymont in Fife, now called St Andrew's.

Philip and James the Less (or 'the younger', also identified as James, the son of Alphaeus) were formerly commemorated (as in the *Book of Common Prayer*) on 1 May, the date of the dedication during the pontificate of John III (561–74) of the church in Rome which contained their relics, originally named after them, but now the basilica of the Holy Apostles (*dei Sancti Apostoli*). To avoid conflict with the optional memorial of St Joseph the Workman, their festival was moved in 1955 to 11 May and in 1969 to 3 May.

Simon, called 'the Cananean' or 'the Zealot' (both titles mean 'zealous'), and Jude (variously 'not Iscariot', 'brother of James', Thaddaeus and Libaeus) share 28 October, possibly the date when their relics were moved to old St Peter's basilica. They are linked because they were said to have been martyred at Suanir in Persia and because St Jerome was of the opinion that they were sons of Mary, wife of Cleopas.

The relics of Bartholomew (identified in the ninth century as Nathanael), who was said to have been flayed alive at Albanopolis (modern Derbend) in Armenia, were taken in 809 from the Lipari islands to Benevento and thence in 983 to Rome. He was included in an early Western martyrology under 24 August, said to be the date when he was beheaded.

The original date (also in the *Book of Common Prayer*) for the feast of Thomas, called Didymus: 'the Twin', reputedly the founder of the Church of the Malabar Christians at Kerala, south-west India, was moved in 1969 from 21 December to 3 July to avoid a festival in Advent. Similarly, so that it should no longer fall in Lent, St Matthias' feast was changed from 24 February to 14 May. Revised Anglican calendars include these changes but allow for commemorations on the traditional dates, if desired.

Stephen

A Greek-speaking Jew, Stephen was one of seven chosen to be an assistant, or 'deacon' (Greek *diakonos*: 'servant') to help in the distribution of alms and food to the widows of the first Hellenistic Christians in Jerusalem. Arraigned before the high priest on a false charge of blasphemy, he so infuriated his judges with his lengthy and cogent defence of his Messianic faith that he was condemned to be stoned to death. Present at his execution was 'a young man named Saul' who would later become the apostle Paul (Ac 6–7).

Early calendars and sermons of Gregory of Nyssa (*c.*330–*c.*395) attest that because Stephen was regarded as the first Christian martyr he was commemorated on 26 December, the day following the Western feast of the Nativity of Christ. Significantly this was also the date of the translation of his relics to Jerusalem in 415, after they had been discovered by a priest called Lucianus at 'Caphar-gamala' (possibly Beit-el-Jamal or Jemmala). This gave rise to the legend that he had been buried by Gamaliel who, although a Pharisee, was thought to have been secretly sympathetic to Christians (Ac 5:34–38).

Eudoxia, married to the western emperor Valentinian III, was present *c.*439 at the dedication of a new shrine on the site of Stephen's martyrdom near the northern gate of the city of Jerusalem. At her request relics were taken from Constantinople to the small church above the catacomb in Rome on the road to Tivoli where St Lawrence (*d.*258), a martyr in deacon's orders, was buried. Near this site Pelagius II (579–90) erected the church of San Lorenzo fuori le Mura (St Lawrence-without-the-Walls). A mosaic on the triumphal arch depicted the pope as donor and St Stephen in the company of other saints. His remains, together with those of St Lawrence, are in the crypt beneath the sanctuary of the basilica, now restored after damage during the Second World War.

Stephen's cult was promoted by the rapid diffusion of his relics which had early earned a reputation for their curative properties. In his *City of God* (413–26) St Augustine of Hippo related (Book XXII:8) the miracles which happened after they were brought to North Africa, including the restoration of a woman's sight after she put to her eyes flowers carried by the bishop who escorted the relics.

Conversion of St Paul

There are three versions of what happened to Paul, born Saul of Tarsus, a strict Pharisee, as he journeyed to Damascus to arrest followers of 'the new way' in the synagogues. One, a third-person narrative, states that as Paul approached the city he was blinded by a light from the sky and fell to the ground as a voice said, 'Saul, Saul, why are you persecuting me?' (Ac 9:3–9). The other two are in Paul's own words: the first delivered as he addressed the crowd after the Roman commander had rescued him from the Jerusalem mob (Ac 22:6–11); the second related in the course of his defence at Caesarea before King Herod Agrippa II (Ac 26:12–18). Despite obvious contradictions in detail (e.g. all heard the disembodied voice, or only Paul heard it; Jesus immediately appointed Paul to preach the Gospel, or the commission came through the agency of Ananias), it is evident that the shattering experience transformed the one-time scourge of the Lord's disciples into the passionate missioner to the gentiles.

Paul's conversion, a feast on 25 January, was originally commemorated only in the Gallican Church. As it was later entered in the so-called Hieronymian Martyrology, composed in the mid-fifth century, as *translatio*: 'translation', it is possible that this date was adopted in Rome to coincide with the removal of some of Paul's relics to the church which stood on the site of the present magnificent basilica of San Paolo fuori le Mura (St Paul's-without-the-Walls).

All Saints' Day

On this day, 1 November, a solemnity, known in England as All-Hallows, or Hallowmas (Old English: *haelou*: 'saint'), are commemorated all those martyrs, known and unknown, who in heaven enjoy the beatific vision of God. In the West the festival was at first celebrated in Rome on 13 May, the date when Boniface IV in 609/10, having received it as a gift from the Byzantine Emperor Phocas, reconsecrated and dedicated 'to the Blessed Mary, ever virgin, mother of all saints', the Pantheon, the magnificent rotunda, a temple 'to all the gods', reconstructed by Hadrian (117–38). The legend that Boniface ordered twenty-eight cartloads of martyrs' bones to be transported there from the catacombs is without foundation.

The present date, for reasons unexplained (it was not a pagan festival), was chosen by Gregory III (731–41) for the dedication 'to the Saviour and his Holy Mother' of a chapel in St Peter's basilica. In it he placed, according to the record, 'the relics of the holy apostles, all saints, martyrs and all the just everywhere'. As a feast of All Saints it had replaced 13 May by the end of the century when Arno, first archbishop of Salzburg, was congratulated by his master and friend, Alcuin of York, then abbot of St Martin's at Tours, on having it adopted by a council assembled at Reisbach in 789. It became general in the French realms of Louis I the Pious in the time of Gregory IV (827–44) and was also known at an early period in England. The intention of the feast was beautifully expressed in the Sarum Missal: 'Almighty everlasting God who hast granted us to venerate the merits of all saints on one day, we beseech thee to bestow upon us the longed-for abundance of thy propitiation, our intercessors having been multiplied.'

All Souls' Day: Commemoration of the Faithful Departed

Amalarius of Metz (*c*.780–850), the liturgical scholar whose intention it was to harmonize Gallican and Roman rites, explained in his treatise *On the Offices of the Church* that he had included an Office for the Dead after All Saints' Day, 'because many pass out of this world without at once being admitted to the company of the blessed'. In this way he expressed, without saying what happened to them, the innate feeling that most Christians, 'saints' in the Pauline sense, are rarely sufficiently good or bad either to be damned or to go immediately to heaven.

Their fate after death, when they face particular or individual judgment, pending the final judgment of all at the end of time, was clarified at the Second General Council of Lyons (1274) when it was said that the souls of those who, being truly repentant, die in charity 'before having satisfied by worthy fruits of penance for their sins of commission and omission', are cleansed after death 'by purgatorial and purifying penalties'. It was further stated that the living would alleviate the suffering of the dead, and help them ultimately to enter God's presence, 'by the sacrifice of the Mass, prayers, alms and other works of piety'. This was the doctrinal confirmation of the medieval practice of celebrating a private Mass, said by a priest attended by a server, with or without people present, on behalf of a departed friend or member of the family.

The annual commemoration of these faithful departed on 2 November (now an optional memorial), the date advocated by Amalarius, was promoted by the influential Benedictine Order in the time of Odilo, abbot of the monastery at Cluny, near Mâcon, Burgundy. In his *City of God* (413–

26), St Augustine of Hippo had claimed that purgation, or cleansing, of the souls of the dead was by fire. This was confirmed for the Middle Ages by an incident related by a monk called Jotsuald, shortly after Odilo's death in 1049, and repeated by St Peter Damian (1007–72). On a rocky islet, a pilgrim returning from the Holy Land encountered a hermit who entrusted him with a message for Odilo from souls confined 'where a blazing fire spits with great violence'. Each day they endured fresh tortures devised by a host of demons. They begged the abbot and his monks to intensify their prayers, vigils and alms-giving so that they would be delivered from their torments.

Moved by compassion, and giving new life to Amalarius' proposed festival, Odilo ordered that on 2 November Masses should be said for the repose of souls in purgatory in all monasteries under his jurisdiction. A bell was to be tolled after Vespers on All Saints' Day, the Office of the Dead recited, and the next morning there was to be a requiem Mass, so named from the first word of the introit, *Requiem aeternam dona eis Domine*: 'Rest eternal grant them, O Lord'. By the thirteenth century this had become common practice throughout the West. In England it was known as early as the archbishopric of Lanfranc (*c.*1010–89) who came to Canterbury, where he rebuilt the cathedral, from Normandy, where he had been prior of the famous abbey of Bec.

The text adduced to justify prayers for the dead, 'All men . . . betook themselves unto prayer and besought him that the sin committed might be wholly put out of remembrance' (2 M 12:41–2), came from one of the four *Books of the Maccabees* which the Reformers said was to be read 'for instruction of manners' but not to establish doctrine. They also rejected the doctrine of purgatory as without biblical foundation. All Souls' Day was therefore excluded from their calendars. The response of the Council of Trent at its twenty-fifth session (1563) was to reaffirm the existence of purgatory. Pius IV, a year later, in his *Profession of Faith*, steadfastly held '. . . that the souls detained there are helped by acts of intercession by the faithful'. The day, with its prayer that the Mass offered may 'bring peace and forgiveness to our brothers and sisters who have died', and that they may be brought to the fullness of eternal glory', thus continues to be observed, although purgation by fire is no longer part of official teaching. Many churches in the Anglican Communion, without accepting the concept of purgatory, also keep 2 November as the Commemoration of (All) the Faithful Departed, stressing Isaiah's prophecy that the heavenly banquet is prepared for all peoples and, Death destroyed for ever, 'the Lord will wipe away the tears from every cheek' (Is 25:6–9).

When Benedict XV was secretary to the Papal Nuncio in Madrid, he noted in Spain the practice, confirmed in 1748, whereby a priest was permitted to say up to three Masses in one day because of the number of the dead to be accommodated. As pope, appalled by the slaughter of the First World War and mindful of the many who had died without the comfort of the last rites, he gave permission on 10 August 1915 for a priest to say three Masses on All Souls' Day, one for souls in purgatory, one for the pope's intention, and one for the priest's.

St Michael and All Angels

In heaven, in communion with holy persons on earth, are the angels. Chief among them is the archangel Michael, the standard-bearer, depicted in art with a sword as he slays the dragon, or holding the scales on which good deeds are weighed against the bad. He had also the power to intercede for souls and to lead them out of hell. His formal cult, which began in the East where the Emperor Constantine built a church in his honour near Constantinople, spread to the West after he appeared in the fifth century on Monte Gargano, Italy (commemorated locally on 8 May). His appearance at Mont-Saint-Michel in Normandy (*f.d.*16 October) led to the foundation there in 996 of a Benedictine monastery. He was also seen in the eighth century on St Michael's Mount in Cornwall.

His feast, Michaelmas Day, on 29 September, commemorates the dedication of a church in Rome in his honour. The additional title 'and all angels' was added to the English calendar in 1549. In the *Roman Calendar* (1969) two other archangels, Gabriel, the angel of the Annunciation, and Raphael, patron of doctors because he moved the waters of the healing pool (Jn 5:1–4), are included in the feast.

Days of Special Prayer and Thanksgiving

I N THE OLD LATIN SERVICE BOOKS AND CALEN-dars Mondays to Fridays were called ferial days, a curious misnomer because in classical times *feria* was literally a rest-day. The explanation may be that each of these days was considered as a festival dedicated to the Lord. Two of these weekdays, Wednesdays and Fridays, were given special emphasis. According to *The Teaching of the Twelve Apostles*, orthodox Christians, by observing them, distinguished themselves from others, uncharitably called 'hypocrites', who fasted on Mondays and Thursdays, like devout Jews. Possibly they were dissemblers who persisted in following the official Jewish calendar, whereas mainstream Christians, like the people of Qumrân who left the Dead Sea Scrolls, observed the calendar of the *Book of Jubilees* and fasted on Wednesdays and Fridays. Later, when this conflict had receded, those two days were given symbolic meaning, Wednesday being associated with Judas' treachery, and Friday with Christ's passion.

The Litany

At the time of the Reformation, certain Wednesdays and Fridays, as well as being commended for fasting or abstinence, were also, in England, days on which the Litany was ordered to be said or sung in procession. The word is derived from the Greek for 'supplication' and is used for a form of prayer in which the congregation responds to petitions made by a priest, deacon or other leader. Examples in the Roman Catholic Church are the Litany of the Saints whose intercessions are invoked, and the Litany of Loreto in which the Blessed Virgin Mary is asked to pray for the faithful. The English Litany was composed by Thomas Cranmer, archbishop of Canterbury, and published in 1544 in response to a command from Henry VIII who, 'plagued with most cruel wars' with Scotland and France, sought divine aid and ordered 'certain godly prayers and suffrages in our native English tongue' to be said in all churches.

Revised, these were eventually incorporated in the *Book of Common Prayer* and after further revision were recited in most parish churches, usually after Morning Prayer on Sundays, the minister kneeling at a litany desk because of the royal injunction of 1547 against processions in church. Despite its majestic phrasing and the beautiful so-called concluding 'Prayer of St Chrysostom', some of the petitions in the Litany, which reflect a past social order, are obsolete. Versions reflecting contemporary concerns are therefore available in Churches of the Anglican Communion – for example, the Great Litany and other litanies in the *American Prayer Book*.

Rogation Days

Three days of intercession, prayer and fasting on Monday, Tuesday and Wednesday before Ascension Day (now removed from the general Roman Calendar and left to local decision), called Rogation Days (from the Latin *rogatio* which translated the Greek word for 'litany'), originally had a penitential, Lenten character. Ashes were imposed and clergy and people, asperged, or sprinkled, with holy water, processed from church to church, along streets and through fields, barefoot and in sackcloth, chanting psalms and the Litany of the Saints. Choice of these three days was attributed to St Mamertus (*d.c.*475), archbishop of Vienne in Gaul, who, when earthquakes followed by fires spread terror among the people, prescribed suitable petitions to avert the recurrence of these catastrophes and to free the countryside from ravaging wolves. The appointed days also coincided with the season when, according to St Sidonius Apollinaris (*c.*423–*c.*480), country people made 'vague supplications for showers and fine weather' for the germination of their newly sown crops.

When these days were adopted in Rome, they were included in a rogatory category together with an existing procession which took place on 25 April, later St Mark's Day, when anciently the Romans propitiated Robigus, the god who averted red mildew from crops, by sacrificing a rust-coloured dog and a sheep at his sanctuary at the fifth milestone on the Via Claudia. Significantly, the Christian procession followed only part of the route, turning at the Milvian bridge towards St Peter's basilica where the concluding Mass was held.

In England these days, called in the *Anglo-Saxon Chronicle* and in the Laws of Athelstan *gang daegas*: 'walking days', served the additional purpose of 'beating the bounds', the demarcation of parish boundaries by beating the limits with willow rods. The custom of 'bumping' the posteriors of choir boys at selected points may be a merciful mitigation of an ancient fertility rite.

Ember Days

According to the *Book of the Pontiffs*, Calistus (217–22) decreed 'that on Saturdays three times a year in the fourth, seventh and tenth months [that is June, September and December, the year then beginning in March] there should be a fast from corn, wine and oil according to the prophecy'. Actually the Lord God told Zechariah (Zc 8:19) that there should also be one in the fifth month, but as the three mentioned coincided with ancient Roman agricultural festivals, Calistus undoubtedly wished to provide Christian alternatives. It was also necessary to counter New Year celebrations which by the fourth century had acquired much of the licentiousness associated with the Saturnalia which began on 17 December. The addition of a fast in Lent, mentioned in a sermon of St Leo I (440–61), completed the 'Fasts of Four Seasons', approximately at the summer and winter solstices and the spring and autumn equinoxes.

In England these fasts became known as Ember Days (late Old English *ymbrendagas*, related to *ymbryne*: 'a period, or season', but *not* connected with the word for 'ashes'). About the beginning of the twelfth century they were observed on Wednesday, Friday and Saturday after the first Sunday in Lent, Pentecost, 14 September and 13 December. The austerity of these seasons made them appropriate times for the ordination of priests and deacons. In the Church of England, Petertide, the Sunday nearest to St Peter's Day (29 June), and Michaelmas (29 September) are now favoured for this ceremony.

Dedication Festival

Church buildings are dedicated to the service of God by solemn consecration in the course of a special ceremony (or within the Mass) at which a bishop presides. With the consent of the Convocations, Henry VIII in 1536 ordered that the Feast of Dedication should be kept 'throughout this realm' of England on the first Sunday in October, an injunction still followed if the date of consecration is not known. This anniversary is distinct from the patronal festival on the feast day of the tutelary saint who is the patron, or protector, of the church named in his honour.

Dedication of the Lateran basilica

Near the walls of the ancient city of Rome, away from the centre, dominated by pagan temples and therefore shunned by the Christian community, in 312 the Emperor Constantine ordered the demolition of the barracks of the imperial horse guards, built on land which Nero had confiscated from the Laterani family. There arose the church originally dedicated to the Saviour but rededicated by Sergius III (904–11) and now known as San Giovanni in Laterano, or the Lateran, the cathedral of Rome, one of the four great basilicas of that city. The festival of its dedication (a feast on 9 November in the Roman Calendar) is kept in thanksgiving for 'the church that is our mother'.

Harvest Thanksgiving

One of the best attended of all church services, of whatever denomination, is the Harvest Festival, responding as it does, even in a secular and industrial age, to an innate feeling that thanks should be rendered 'for all good gifts around us'. Urban congregations who have never handled agricultural machinery, sing, in churches decorated with fruit and flowers, 'We plough the fields and scatter the good seed on the land', a German hymn composed by Matthias Claudius (1740–1815). In compensation, 'the fruits of the earth' is in some places given a broad interpretation and mechanical products are displayed.

In England 1 August (St Peter in Chains in the Roman Calendar) was known as Lammas (Old English *hlafmaese*: 'loaf festival'), when bread from the first corn to ripen was brought to church to be blessed. No provision was made for this service in the *Book of Common Prayer*, although the date was retained as a Black Letter Day. 'Harvest homes', feasting after the sheaves were brought in, nevertheless remained a folk festival and in 1843 R.S. Hawker, Vicar of Morwenstow, Cornwall, tried to restore a religious meaning by using bread made from the ripe corn during a special Sunday Eucharist. Its popularity spread and Harvest Thanksgiving figures in most modern service books. In the United States it coincides with Thanksgiving Day (the fourth Thursday in November), recalling the gratitude of the first settlers in Virginia and Massachusetts for their survival from the threat of starvation.

Festival of Nine Lessons and Carols

To meet modern needs, special days have been appointed, for example 'For the Unity of Christians' and 'For Peace and Justice'. An extra-liturgical occasion, popular in schools and colleges at the end of the term before Christmas, is the Festival of Nine Lessons and Carols. It dates from 1880 when E.W. Benson, then first bishop of Truro, Cornwall, and later archbishop of Canterbury, arranged it in the hope that it would keep people out of the beer shops on Christmas Eve. Adopted in 1918 by the chapel of King's College, Cambridge, it was one of the first services to be broadcast in the early days of public wireless transmission and, televised, is now considered an essential part of Christmas celebrations.

Stations of the Cross

An assembly of the faithful at a 'station' (Latin *statio*: 'fixed place') on 'station days', usually Wednesdays and Fridays, was characterized by a fast from noon until three in the afternoon, followed by a eucharistic service. In accordance with the custom said to have begun during the papacy of St Gregory the Great, popes went in procession to certain 'station churches', among them Santa Maria Maggiore, Santa Sabina and St John Lateran. Until 1970 these 'station days' were marked in the Missal so that the faithful could associate themselves with them in spirit.

The devotion known as Stations of the Cross, practised on Fridays in Lent but not necessarily restricted to that season, originated in Jerusalem where pilgrims paused for prayer and meditation at points along the Via Dolorosa ('Sorrowful Road') associated with incidents in Jesus' progress from Pilate's praetorium to Calvary. Crusaders returning from the Holy Land may have made this devotion known in the West but the main agents were the Franciscans who had been given custody of the Holy Places in 1342. Crosses, tableaux, carvings or pictures now denote the stations on a simulated route, either outside or within church precincts.

The number of stations varied (as many as thirty-six at one period) but they were fixed in 1731 at fourteen in the so-called 'Clementine Instruction' of Clement XII. They are: Jesus is condemned to death; receives the cross; falls for the first time; meets his mother; is relieved of the cross by Simon of Cyrene; Veronica wipes his face; he falls for the second time; the women of Jerusalem weep for him; he falls for the third time; is stripped of his garments; nailed to the cross; yields up his spirit; is taken down; and placed in the tomb. A fifteenth station is now added: 'the Resurrection of Jesus from the dead', thus re-emphasizing the essential truth that 'as in Adam all die, even so in Christ shall all be made alive' (I Cor 15:22).

Associated with the devotion is the hymn *Stabat Mater Dolorosa*, of unknown authorship but ascribed among others to Jacopone da Todi (*c*.1230–1306), the Franciscan poet. Rendered into English by various hands as 'At the Cross her station keeping,/Stood the mournful Mother weeping', it encourages the devotee to share Mary's grief but to hope for salvation through Christ's sacrificial death. Of musical settings, many intended for concert performance, perhaps the best known are those by Josquin, Palestrina, Haydn, Schubert, Liszt, Verdi and Stanford.

Liturgical Colours

Principal holy days · Select Bibliography

Glossary · Index

Liturgical Colours

THE SEQUENCE OF COLOURS associated with seasons and festivals in the Roman Catholic calendar is based on the rubrics of the missal approved by St Pius V in 1570, confirmed by the *Ordo Missae* of 1969. Five colours are permitted: white, red, green, violet and black. Should these colours have undesirable or contrary symbolic associations in the mission field, the regional conference of bishops may change them.

Roman Catholic practice, with some degree of latitude, is followed in Anglican churches where colour is accepted as an aid to worship:

1. Sundays 'of the year' and ordinary weekdays: green.
2. Advent and Lent: violet (or blue or black).
   Rose pink may be used on the Third Sunday in Advent and the Fourth Sunday in Lent.
3. Christmas, Epiphany, Holy Thursday (Chrism Mass and Mass of the Lord's Supper), Easter, Trinity Sunday: white (or gold).
4. Passion Sunday: red (or rose).
5. Pentecost: red.
6. Solemnities of the Lord (other than Passion Sunday): white (or gold).
7. Apostles, evangelists and martyrs: red (but St John, Apostle and Evangelist [27 December]; Conversion of St Paul [25 January]; Chair of St Peter [22 February] and the Nativity of St John the Baptist: white).
8. Angels, saints who are not martyrs and the feast of All Saints: white (or yellow).
9. Commemoration of All the Faithful Departed: violet (or black).

Principal Holy Days

JANUARY

1 *Solemnity of Mary, Mother of God: Naming of Jesus*
6 *Epiphany*
Sunday after 6 January: *Baptism of the Lord*
25 *Conversion of Paul, Apostle*

FEBRUARY

2 *Presentation of the Lord*
11 *Our Lady of Lourdes*
22 *Chair of Peter, Apostle*

MARCH

17 *Patrick*
19 *Joseph, Husband of Mary*
25 *Annunciation of the Lord*

APRIL

23 *George, Martyr*
25 *Mark, Evangelist*

MAY

1 *Joseph the Workman*
3 *Philip and James, Apostles*
14 *Matthias, Apostle*
31 *Visitation of the Blessed Virgin Mary*
First Sunday after Pentecost: *Holy Trinity*
Thursday after Holy Trinity: *Corpus Christi: Thanksgiving for the institution of Holy Communion*

Friday after the second Sunday after Pentecost: *Sacred Heart of Jesus*
Saturday after the second Sunday after Pentecost: *Immaculate Heart of Mary*

JUNE

24 *The birth of John the Baptist*
29 *Peter and Paul, Apostles*

JULY

3 *Thomas, Apostle*
16 *Our Lady of Mount Carmel*
22 *Mary Magdalene*
25 *James, Apostle*

AUGUST

5 *Dedication of Santa Maria Maggiore*
6 *The Transfiguration of Our Lord*
15 *Assumption of the Blessed Virgin Mary*
22 *Queenship of Mary*
24 *Bartholomew, Apostle*
29 *Beheading of John the Baptist*

SEPTEMBER

8 *Birthday of the Blessed Virgin Mary*
14 *Triumph of the Holy Cross*
15 *Our Lady of Sorrow*

21 *Matthew, Apostle and
Evangelist*
29 *Michael, Gabriel, and
Raphael, Archangels: St Michael
and All Angels: Michaelmas*

OCTOBER

 7 *Our Lady of the Rosary*
18 *Luke the Evangelist*
28 *Simon and Jude, Apostles*

NOVEMBER

 1 *All Saints*
 2 *All Souls: Commemoration of
the Faithful Departed*
 9 *Dedication of St John Lateran*
21 *Presentation of the Blessed
Virgin*

30 *Andrew, Apostle*
Last Sunday of the liturgical
year: *Christ the Universal King*

DECEMBER

 8 *The Immaculate Conception of
the Blessed Virgin Mary:
Birthday of St Mary the Virgin*
24 *Vigil of Christmas:
Christmas Eve*
25 *Christmas*
26 *Stephen, the first martyr*
27 *John, Apostle and Evangelist*
28 *Holy Innocents*
Sunday within the octave of
Christmas (or 30 December, if
there is no Sunday): *The Holy
Family*

Select Bibliography

LISTED BELOW are works to which the present writer is greatly indebted. It should be noted that the history of festivals in the first eight centuries continues to be the subject of revision. Only books in English are cited: if translated the date of the latest available edition is given.

Chapters on the Christian calendar were included in the past in histories of the liturgy, notably L. Duchesne: *Christian Worship. Its Origins and Evolution*, 5th edition, London, 1923, and Dom Gregory Dix: *The Shape of the Liturgy*, London, 1945 (reprinted with notes by P. Marshall, New York, 1982). A work which may be said to have initiated the independent study of the subject and to have given it a name was K.A. Heinrich Kellner: *Heortology. A History of Christian Festivals from their Origin to the Present Day*, London, 1908, full of interest but now to be used with caution. Since then much has been added: W.H. Frere: *Studies in the Early Roman Liturgy: I. The Kalendar*, London, 1930; J.W. Tyrer: *Historical Survey of Holy Week. Its Services and Ceremonial*, London, 1932; A.A. McArthur: *The Evolution of the Christian Year*, London, 1953; N.M. Denis-Boulet: *The Christian Calendar*, London, 1960; and W. Rordorf: *Sunday*, London, 1968.

Modern studies are: A.G. Martinmort: *The Church at Prayer. Volume IV: The Liturgy and Time*, London, 1985, incorporating Second Vatican Council reforms; various contributions to W. Vos and G. Wainwright (eds.): *Liturgical Time*, London, 1982; and Thomas J. Talley: *The Origins of the Liturgical Year*, New York, 1986. A scholarly summary of the present position (and basic references) is Peter G. Cobb, 'History of the Christian Year', in Paul Bradshaw, Geoffrey Wainwright and Edward Yarnold (eds.): *The Study of Liturgy*, new edition, London, 1991. J. Wilkinson: *Egeria's Travels*, London, 1971, extensively annotated, is filled with information on the liturgy in Jerusalem.

Of interest are articles in *The New Catholic Encyclopedia*, New York, 1966; J.G. Davies (ed.): *A New Dictionary of Liturgy and Worship*, London,

1986; and, in a lighter vein, J.C.J. Metford: *Christian Lore and Legend*, London and New York, 1983. An essential work of reference is F.L. Cross and E.A. Livingstone (eds.): *The Oxford Dictionary of the Christian Church*, revised, Oxford, 1983. Non-canonical writings are to be found in E. Hennecke: *New Testament Apocrypha*, 2 vols, London, 1963.

The best edition of the *Liber Pontificalis* is Raymond Davies: *The Book of the Pontiffs*, Liverpool, 1989. Extracts of documents and other material relating to the history of the Church to 337 are to be found in J. Stevenson: *A New Eusebius*, new edition, revised by W.H.C. Frend, London, 1987.

Biblical references may be pursued in the following translations:
1. King James' Bible, the so-called 'Authorized Version' (actually 'Appointed to be read in Churches'), because of the beauty of its phrasing.
2. *The New Jerusalem Bible* (1985). Scholarly and closest to the originals.
3. *The Revised English Bible* (1989). Accurate, embodying the best of recent scholarship, modern but not colloquial.

Glossary

An asterisk (*) indicates an essential cross-reference

absolution

The formal act in the *sacrament of penance by which a priest, using the formula 'I absolve you' (Latin *absolvere*: 'to free from'), or praying that God may absolve a person or the congregation, pronounces the forgiveness of sins by Christ.

abstinence

Refraining for a day or a season from certain kinds of food or drink, as opposed to *fasting which limits the quantity taken, e.g., to one main meal a day. Ash Wednesday, Good Friday and Fridays in Lent are recommended but another form of penance may be substituted for reasons of health or age.

acolyte

A person (Greek *akolouthos*: 'attendant') who assists a priest or deacon or has other duties, such as carrying candles in a procession.

Acts of Pilate

A work not composed before the fourth century which claims to be the record of Jesus' trial and crucifixion.

agape

Greek for (Christian) love for one's fellows. In the early Church expressed in the form of a shared meal, later suppressed because it tended to create disciplinary problems. It has now been revived for limited use in connection with the *Eucharist.

alleluia

From the Hebrew for 'praise ye Yahweh', a joyful acclamation said or sung in the *Divine Office and before the reading of the *gospel in the *Eucharist. In Lent it is replaced by a *tract.

altar

The consecrated table, either movable or fixed (usually of natural stone), on which the *Eucharist is celebrated. It should be free standing so that the *president may *cense it as he walks around it, and face the congregation as he celebrates the Eucharist.

angelus

A devotion in honour of the incarnation of Christ, so named from the opening word in Latin, *Angelus Domini nuntiavit Mariae*: 'the angel of the Lord declared unto Mary', recalling Gabriel's words at the annunciation to the Blessed Virgin. During the season of Easter it is replaced by the prayer *Regina Coeli Laetare*: 'Queen of Heaven, rejoice'.

Anglican
Pertaining to the Church of England.

Anglican Communion
Those Churches which are in communion with the *see of Canterbury, i.e., they have a common liturgical and theological tradition and recognize each others' orders as valid. (Women priests are exceptional.)

Anglo-Catholicism
Within the Church of England a movement which emphasizes continuity of the *Catholic tradition within the reformed Church. (See *Oxford Movement.)

anthem
The English form of *antiphon, now used for sacred vocal music.

antiphon
A psalm or hymn, strictly sung alternately by two choirs but now equivalent to *anthem. An entrance antiphon, the text varying according to the day or season, may be sung at the beginning of *Mass.

apocrypha
(i) Those books of the Greek Old Testament which were not included in the Hebrew bible. An alternative name is deuterocanonical. (ii)

Writings, e.g., *Acts of Pilate, *Book of James, which were not received into the *canon and because of their fanciful contents gave rise to the adjective 'apocryphal', meaning untrue or of doubtful authenticity.

Arianism
A heresy named after its proponent Arius (*c.*250–*c.*336) which denied that Jesus Christ was truly God.

asperse
To sprinkle with holy water in the ceremony known as asperges, or sprinkling.

Ave Maria
The first Latin words of the Angelic Salutation, 'Hail Mary, full of grace' (Lk 1:28), on which is based a form of prayer to the Blessed Virgin Mary.

baptism
The *sacrament in which, in the name of the Father, Son and Holy Spirit, by immersion or sprinkling of water a person is cleansed of all sin, reborn and sanctified in Christ to everlasting life. The *rite, administered at the font (or receptacle for holy water) in the baptistery (the portion of a church set aside for the ceremony) admits the candidate to the Christian Church.

basilica
From the Latin *basilicus*: 'royal', 'noble'. In ancient Rome a public hall, adapted for Christian worship after Christianity was recognized

legally. The name is now given to eleven principal churches in Rome, and to others so designated, as a title of honour.

beatification
The papal declaration that a deceased person, having lived a holy life (and died a martyr's death in many cases), is now in heaven and is to be called 'Blessed'. It may be a stage towards *canonization.

bishop
From the Greek *episkopos*: 'overseer', a successor to the Apostles, consecrated by fellow bishops by laying hands on his head and invoking the Holy Spirit.

Black Letter days
Lesser festivals and saints' days, printed in black in the calendar of the *Book of Common Prayer*.

Blessed Sacrament
The *Eucharist, also the consecrated bread which is 'reserved', kept for the communion of the sick.

Book of James
A non-canonical or *apocryphal writing, possibly as early as the second century, which relates the infancy of Jesus. Also known as the *Protevangelium*: 'the Gospel before the Gospel', the name given by G. Postel to his Latin translation (1552).

Breviary
The liturgical book containing the *Divine Office. From the Latin *breviarium*: 'abridgement' because it combined selected material in one book.

bull
A solemn papal letter, so-called because of the leaden seal (Latin *bulla*) attached to it. It is named after the opening Latin words.

canonical
From the Latin for 'rule' or 'standard'. Those biblical books accepted as divinely inspired.

canonization
The papal declaration that a deceased person, previously granted *beatification, may be included in the canon, or catalogue, of saints.

canticle
A sacred chant from the Bible, other than a psalm.

catechumen
One who is being instructed (Greek *katekhouminos*) in the faith previous to *baptism. The period of instruction is known as the catechumenate.

Catholic
(i) From Latin *catholicus*. 'universal', first used by St Ignatius (35–107). The Christian faith believed 'everywhere, always and by all' (Vincent of Lérins).
(ii) Those who accept the Apostolic succession of *bishops and *priests and the place of the Bible and *tradition in faith and worship. Roman Catholics are in communion with the pope in Rome; the Church of England claims to be 'Catholic and Reformed'.

celebrant

A *priest or *bishop who presides at the *Eucharist.

cense

To perfume and sanctify an *altar, sacred object or a congregation with incense burned in a censer, a metal container suspended by chains, also called a thurible and carried in procession by a thurifer.

chalice

From Latin *calix*: 'cup', a vessel to contain wine consecrated at the *Eucharist.

chancel

Originally a screen (Latin *cancellus*) which divided the *choir where the *clergy sat from the *nave, now called the *sanctuary.

Charlemagne

Charles the Great (*c*.742–814) who became the first Holy Roman Emperor on Christmas Day, 800. He promoted liturgical reforms.

choir

(i) That part of a church reserved for the clergy. (ii) In monasteries the stalls where the *Divine Office is chanted. (iii) The body of singers who perform the vocal music of the service.

church

(i) The building where the faithful assemble for worship. (ii) Church (a) all baptized Christians. (b) divisions of the Church, e.g., *Anglican, *Episcopal, *Orthodox, *Roman Catholic.

clergy

*Bishops, *priests and *deacons ordained for the sacred ministry and thus set apart from the *laity.

collect

Literally an 'assembly', it came to mean a prayer which brings together, or expresses, thoughts relevant to the occasion.

communion

(i) Holy Communion, the *eucharistic rite. (ii) Reception of the consecrated *elements. (iii) Those who share a common faith and practice, e.g., *Anglican Communion. (iv) Communion of Saints: the spiritual union in Christ of all Christians, whether in Heaven, Purgatory or on earth.

consecration

The act of making holy, or separating for divine use, a thing or person. Also the ritual act by which bread and wine become the Body and Blood of Christ.

Constantine the Great

Roman emperor (*d*.337) who made Christianity a tolerated religion and summoned the *Council of Nicaea (325). He rebuilt as his capital the Greek city of Byzantium, named Constantinople after him (330).

council

A convocation of *bishops and prelates of the Church, either provincial or oecumenical (i.e., 'universal'). Seven of the latter (up to the Second Council of

Nicaea in 787) are recognized by *East and *West: fourteen more by the Roman Catholic Church.

Counter Reformation
The period of Roman Catholic revival inaugurated by the Council of Trent (1545–63). One aim was to counter the spread of *Protestantism but more positive aspects were the reform of the Church and the renewal of its spiritual life and mission.

Cranmer, Thomas (1489–1556)
Archbishop of Canterbury (1553–55), responsible for the formulation of the liturgy in English and the first Prayer Book (1549). Accused of heresy in the reign of Mary Tudor, when there was a return to the old religion, he recanted on many issues under threat of death but later renounced his recantation and was burned at the stake in Oxford (21 March, his feast day in the *Alternative Service Book*).

creed
From the first Latin word *credo*: 'I believe'. A statement of faith, originally made by candidates for *baptism. At *Mass on Sundays and *solemnities the creed based on the teaching of the Council of Nicaea (325) and finalized by the Council of Constantinople (381) now begins 'We believe' as it is an affirmation by the whole congregation.

crucifix
A cross bearing the image of Christ.

deacon
An ordained *minister who assists the *priest, reads the *gospel and may preach, confer *baptism and solemnize marriage.

Dead Sea Scrolls
Fragments and manuscripts composed *c*.170 BC–68 AD, found from 1947 onwards in caves near Qumrân on the Dead Sea, the site of an ascetic Messianic community.

Diaspora
Judaic communities dispersed throughout the Mediterranean and Asia Minor.

diocese
The administrative area over which a *bishop exercises jurisdiction.

Divine Office
Psalms, hymns, prayers, biblical and spiritual readings for use at the canonical *Hours, printed in the Breviary, revised 1970 onwards. Also known as the Liturgy of the *Hours.

dogma
From the Greek for 'declaration'. Doctrine taught by the Church as revealed truth and therefore to be believed by all the faithful.

East
A convenient way to refer to *Orthodox Churches which separated from Rome in 1054, although temporarily reunited in 1274 and 1439.

elements
Bread and wine consecrated at the *Eucharist.

encyclical
A papal document circulated to the people, setting out the mind of the pope on a particular issue.

Episcopal
Churches of the *Anglican Communion, e.g., in the USA and Scotland, so named because they are ruled by *bishops (Latin: *episcopi*).

epistle
A passage from one of the New Testament letters read at a divine service.

Eucharist
The central act of Christian worship, also called the *Mass, Holy *Communion and the *Lord's Supper.

evangelical
Applied to *Anglicans who hold that the scriptures alone are the standard for faith and conduct. They stress the need for conversion, belief in the atoning work of Christ, social concern and the avoidance of excessive ceremonial in worship.

Evangelists
The writers of the four canonical *Gospels.

Exodus
The release of the Israelites from servitude in Egypt, and the name of the book which tells the story of divine intervention which enabled them 'to go out' to the Promised Land.

fast
Restricting food, e.g., to one meal a day, as opposed to *abstinence from certain foods.

father
(i) A title given to *priests and *deacons who by their calling are 'fathers in God', spiritual counsellors of the faithful.
(ii) Fathers of the Church are saintly writers of the first centuries.

feast
A day set apart for commemoration or for rendering special honour, e.g., Sundays; moveable feasts (Easter, Pentecost); fixed (Christmas, Epiphany) and saints' days. In the Roman Catholic calendar, a commemoration of lesser importance than a *solemnity but greater than a *memorial. Feasts of obligation are those which all are obliged to observe by attending *Mass (e.g. Feast of the Annunciation).

font
A receptacle for holy water for the rite of *baptism, often placed at the entrance of a church to symbolize acceptance into the faith.

Gallican rite
Services which prevailed in Gaul (with resemblances in Milan and Spain) from the fourth to the eighth centuries.

gentiles
The name given to 'nations' (Latin *gentes*) of non-Jews and later to non-Christians.

'Gloria in excelsis Deo'
The first Latin words of the hymn 'Glory to God in the highest', used on Sundays (but not in Advent or Lent) after the act of penance, in thanksgiving for *absolution from sin.

Golgotha
From the Aramaic for 'skull', the equivalent of Calvary (Latin *calvarium*), the place where Jesus was crucified, explained as a mount which resembled a skull; or where criminals were executed; or where Adam's skull was thought to be buried.

gospel
The 'good news' (Old English *godspel*), a passage from one of the four canonical Gospels read at a divine service.

heresy
Teaching or belief of a sect (Greek *hairesis*) which is contrary to officially defined doctrine.

Holy Spirit
The third person of the Holy Trinity, distinct from the Father and the Son but coequal and coeternal.

hosanna
A shout of joy (Hebrew *ho-shi-a-na*: 'Save me'), taken from the Psalms.

Host
Bread consecrated at the *Eucharist (Latin *hostia*: 'sacrificial victim'), the Body and Blood of Christ, 'the full, perfect and sufficient sacrifice'.

Hours
The five canonical hours of the *Divine Office, or Liturgy of the Hours, so named because they are recited or sung at appointed hours.

icon
An image (Greek *eikón*) but particularly a sacred picture of the *Orthodox Churches.

introit
The entrance hymn and introductory rite at the *Mass.

Jubilees, Book of
An alternative Aramaic (or possibly Hebrew) version of the Creation and *Exodus *c.*100 BC. It advocated a solar calendar.

laity
Members of the congregation who are not in Holy Orders.

Lateran
The residence which belonged to Plautius Lateranus in the time of Nero and was given as a residence by Emperor *Constantine to the pope. Adjoining it is the Church of the Most Holy Saviour, known as St John Lateran, the pope's church as bishop of Rome, hence his Cathedral.

lectionary
The book (or list) giving the lessons, or scriptural extracts, to be read as part of the *Ministry of the Word.

liturgy
(i) The official congregational worship of the Church, particularly the *Eucharist. (ii) The form, or *rite, prescribed for that worship, e.g., *Gallic, Roman. The Liturgy of the Word is another name for the *Ministry of the Word.

Lord's Supper, The

The name (I Cor 11:20) for the *Eucharist, preferred by some *Protestants.

Mass

The Catholic name for the *Eucharist, of uncertain derivation but thought to be connected with the concluding formula of 'sending' (Latin *missio*) in which the faithful are told to 'go forth in peace'.

mattins

The *Anglican spelling of 'matins', Morning Prayer, the first of the canonical *Hours.

memorial

In the Roman calendar a festival of lesser importance than a *solemnity.

ministers

In Latin 'servants', in ecclesiastical usage ordained *clergy. Sacred ministers are those who administer the *sacraments.

Ministry of the Word

In the *Mass the part which precedes the liturgy of the *Eucharist and contains scriptural readings, a responsorial psalm and a sermon, or homily.

missal

The book containing material pertaining to the *Mass.

nave

That part of a *church divided from the *sanctuary which is assigned to the *laity.

Octave

The eighth day after a *feast, counting inclusively, and the eight preceding days during which it may be observed.

Office

An authorized form of worship. Also the *Divine Office.

ordination

The laying on of hands with prayer by which a *bishop admits a candidate to the ministry of the Church. (Bishops are *consecrated.)

Orthodox Churches

Independent Churches (Russian, Greek, etc.) in communion with one another, sharing the same faith and recognizing the honorary primacy of the Patriarch of Constantinople. (See *East.)

Oxford Movement

A movement within the Church of England, so called because it dates from 1833 when John Keble (1792–1866) preached the Oxford Assize Sermon in which he condemned state interference in ecclesiastical matters. Its supporters were called Tractarians after J.H. Newman (later Cardinal Newman) published Tract XC which declared that many Catholic practices were not contrary to the spirit of *Anglicanism. It inspired *Anglo-Catholicism.

president

The *celebrant who presides at the *Mass or *Eucharist

priest

The ordained *minister who may preside at the *Eucharist, grant absolution and perform certain other ecclesiastical duties.

proper
Those parts of the religious service which are 'proper', i.e., special to the day or season and are therefore variable, in contrast to the rest of the service which is invariable. A proper preface introduces the main part of the service.

Protestant
Literally those members of the Diet of Speyer (1529) who protested against the decisions of the Catholic majority but now the usual description of those persons and denominations who maintain the principles of the *Reformation, favour the *evangelical approach, and doctrines which are consonant with the scriptures as opposed to *tradition.

quire
The name in the *Book of Common Prayer* for the *choir, the place occupied by singers.

Red Letter days
Major festivals originally printed in red in the *Book of Common Prayer*.

Reformation
The religious, social and political changes of the sixteenth century which divided *Protestant Churches from Roman Catholicism. Although its origins lie in fourteenth-century attacks on abuses and the power of Rome, it is usual to attribute its impetus to the treatises (1520) of Martin Luther (1483–1546).

'Regina Coeli Laetare'
The opening Latin words of the Eastertide anthem 'Queen of Heaven, rejoice', celebrating Christ's resurrection.

rite
Words and actions for the performance of a religious act, e.g., *Mass, *baptism.

Sacrament
Classically defined as 'an outward and visible sign of an inward and spiritual grace', e.g. *baptism. The Blessed Sacrament is the *Eucharist. Also the bread consecrated at the Eucharist.

sacristy
A room in a church where the *clergy put on their *vestments and where liturgical vessels are stored.

sanctuary
The part of a church which contains the *altar, divided by a screen or rails from the *nave.

Sarum, Use of
The name for the Latin *rite used at Salisbury Cathedral from the eleventh century onwards until the *Reformation.

See
Properly a *bishop's seat (Latin *sedes*) or chair (Latin *cathedra*) which stands in his cathedral church, but also used for the territory which he administers.

sentence
Text spoken before the reading of the *gospel.

solemnity
> A feast of the greatest importance, e.g., Sunday, All Saints' Day.

synod
> An assembly of ecclesiastics, at first synonymous with a *council but now a diocesan assembly. The General Synod of the Church of England is composed of *bishops, *clergy and *laity.

tract
> Verse, or verses, or a responsorial psalm, which replace the *alleluia in Lent.

tradition
> That part of the revealed word of God which is not contained in scripture but which is expressed in the accumulated wisdom and teaching of the Church.

typology
> The relationship between a person or event (the 'type' or 'figure') in the Old Testament which prefigures that in the New (the 'antitype'), e.g., Abel's murder: the death of Christ.

unitarianism
> The belief that God is one person, not three in one.

vestments
> Garments worn by the *clergy when exercising their special functions, e.g., administration of the *sacraments.

Vigil
> The day or evening before a great festival. Also a service in preparation for that event.

Vulgate
> From the Latin *Vulgatus*: 'common', 'popular'. The Latin translation of the Bible, mainly by St Jerome, made at the request in 382 of St Damasus I and later revised.

West
> A general term for Churches which originated in the West of Europe, as distinct from those in the *East.

Index of seasons, festivals
and related topics

A

Advent 29–34, 73, 79, 86; wreath
31
All Saints' Day 86, 115–16
All Souls' Day 36, 116–18
Andrew, St 113
Angels, St Michael and all 118
Angelus 88
Anne, St 99, 103, 104
Annunciation of the Lord: to
Mary 34, 76, 88, 89, 90; to
Joseph 34
Apostles 112–13
Ascension of the Lord 15, 23,
69–71, 84
Ash Wednesday 45, 46, 47, 57,
59
Assumption of the BVM 97–9
Ave Maria 88, 101

B

Baptism 42, 53, 68, 72; of the
Lord 73–4, 84
Barnabas, St 112
Bartholomew, St 113
Bernadette, St 90–1
Birth of Jesus 17, 20; date of the
22
Birthday of the BVM 88, 99–100
Body and Blood of Christ 79–82

C

Candlemas 74–6
Carmel, Our Lady of Mt 94–5

Cecilia, St 109
Celebration of the Lord's Passion
63
Childermas 110
Chrism, Blessing of the 59–60
Christ: passim; see Circumcision;
Naming; Transfiguration;
King
Christmas 29, 30, 31; Day 36–8;
Eve 29, 35–6; octave 39
Christmastide 35–42
Circumcision of Christ 39–40, 89
Colours, Liturgical 126
Commemoration of the Faithful
Departed 116–18
Commination, A 27
Communion of Saints 107
Compline 28, 67
Conception of the BVM 105
Confessor 107
Conversion of St Paul 115
Corpus Christi 79–82, 83
Crib, Christmas 35–6
Cross: see Exaltation; Stations;
Veneration

D

Dedication Festival 121
Divine Office 25, 68
Dormition of the BVM 88, 98

E

Easter 14, 20, 23, 30, 35, 42, 45,
54; Day 66–8; octave 68–9;